SPIRITUAL FOOD

VOLUME 1

Convert Your Potential To Product (PO to PRO)

I0181003

CLATIN WILLIAMS

Published by: The Publisher's Notebook Limited

THE PUBLISHER'S
NOTEBOOK LIMITED
PUBLISHERS FOR THE CHRISTIAN GENRE

SPIRITUAL FOOD: VOLUME 1 - Convert Your Potential To Product (PO to PRO)

ISBN: 978-976-96123-0-3

Cover design: Dale Sewell (sewelldale@yahoo.com)

Published by: THE PUBLISHER'S NOTEBOOK LIMITED

THE PUBLISHER'S NOTEBOOK LIMITED
PUBLISHERS FOR THE CHRISTIAN GENRE

publisher@thepublishersnotebook.com

Telephone: (876) 782-1866

DEDICATION

I dedicate this book to my spiritual father Bishop Courtney McLean of Worship and Faith International Fellowship and the Courtney McLean School of Ministry. His vision, ministry and teaching have unlocked my potential to be an author and have helped me to convert my potential into this product.

I dedicate this book to my treasured gift and soulmate, Annakay Williams for her support, encouragement and inspiration.

I dedicate this book to my beloved son Zaire Clatin Williams who loves Jesus and has expressed his desire to be a good boy for God to me at age five. You are a blessing and an inspiration. I pray that the Lord will seal you for His kingdom, order your steps by His Word and use you for His glory.

I dedicate this book to the memory of my beloved grandmother the late, Edith Williams who helped to shape me into the man that I have become through her love, parental training, excellent example and prayers.

I dedicate this book to every believer who loves God and is passionate about His Word and delight in it. To all those who have been inspired by my daily devotions via WhatsApp and Facebook and have encouraged me to publish this book.

TABLE OF CONTENTS

ACKNOWLEDGEMENT

I thank the following persons who have helped and inspired me along the way:

- My spiritual father **Bishop Courtney McLean** for using his prophetic gift to instruct me to do this daily devotion. The Lord had spoken to me prior to that meeting and told me to do the daily devotion and given me this format. I started writing but I did only two devotions and stopped because I didn't think I would be able to do it consistently. When I met with Bishop he confirmed that this was what God wanted me to do by telling me that I need to do a daily devotion. My meeting with him was not about a daily devotion but some other challenge I was dealing with. As a result I was able to overcome my fear and trust God to equip me for that which He has called me to do. Indeed He equips us and gives us Grace to do anything that He has called us to do. I have moved from two devotions to publishing the 1st of 4 volumes of this 90 days daily devotion.

- **Stephanie Tomlinson** for her persistence in encouraging me to write this book and her obedience to God's instruction to bless

i

me with a portion of the publishing fee. One morning I woke up about 3am and went outside to pray. I asked God to send the resources necessary for me to publish my book. By the time I was done praying and went back inside, I got a message from her saying that the Lord spoke to her and told her to give me the money to publish my book. She gave me the money that same day and I went to the publisher the next day and signed the contract. When you pray God will indeed hear you and answer your prayer right away.

- **Rev. Doc Beverly Austin** and **Sis Dionne Smith**, my teachers at the Courtney McLean School of Ministry who equipped me with the tools necessary to interpret the scriptures and organize my testimonies and stories into these powerful messages to impact the lives of so many generations to come.

- My aunt **Marcia Fearon** who has been a mother and a tower of strength to me. She gave me the inspiration to write the first devotion I did, *"God's Healing Power, Still Active!"*

- Last but not least, my wife **Annakay** for her support, encouragement and prayers to help me to complete this book.

FOREWORD

If I was to describe Clatin Williams, I would say he is diligent, articulate, a student of the Word, eager and passionate about empowering and encouraging others in the Word of God. Most importantly he has a strong sense of the calling that is on his life.

Spiritual Food Volume 1 "From Potential to Product" is merely a by-product of the excellence that flows from the life of Clatin. This 90 days devotional can strengthen you, empower you and give you insights.

What I believe sets this devotional apart is the candid testimonies shared that solidify the Power of the Word of God in the lives of the believer. The Word of God says that we overcome by the blood of the lamb and the Word of our testimonies. Therefore what lies within these pages is the Power of God to help you overcome whatever you may be faced with.

In an Era that makes it increasingly difficult to be devoted I am happy that you have picked up this book. Your life is about to be transformed from

PO to PRO (potential to product) as you allow this book to help you in your daily devotion to God.

Bishop Courtney McLean

Founder and Senior Pastor

Worship and Faith International Fellowship (WAFIF)

Author: **Honoring God the Gateway to Success**

Turning Nothing into Something

INTRODUCTION

In 2015 I discovered that I was in a marriage that was not God's Will for my life. I started fasting and praying for God to deliver me and He led me to Worship and Faith International Fellowship. For weeks He kept showing me the number 55 but I couldn't understand why and I kept asking until one morning before going to my previous church, Sandy Bay New Testament in Clarendon, He told me to turn on the television. When I did, I saw Bishop Courtney McLean preaching. I listened until the service was finished and there it was the address, 55 Old Harbour Road.

I visited the church that same week and my life has never been the same since. The Lord instructed me to separate from her and I obeyed. God does not like divorce, but His will must be done in your life. If you are married outside of God's will, I believe that He will forgive you and deliver you so that His will can be done in your life. I explain this more clearly in Days 15 – 17. Two years later I got divorced. Before the process was even complete, He connected me with my soulmate whom I married a year later. I also received prophecies concerning my purpose and call to be a Pastor. I started the journey by enrolling into Preaching 101 at the Courtney McLean School of Ministry. By the time I completed the first module, the Lord told me to start writing this daily devotion and gave me this interesting outline. My Bishop later confirmed this instruction in a meeting.

I believe that this devotion was inspired by God and it will help to transform your life by equipping you with a Word to overcome your daily challenges. All of us are created with the Potential (Po) to be great and to do great things, to become products (Pro). I am a living testimony that you can convert this potential into product, Po to Pro. For most of my school life I hated the subject English because of the reading and writing. I would prefer to work with numbers on any given day but interestingly I later discovered that I actually have the potential to be a writer. Not only did I discover but I activated this Potential and developed it into this product you are now reading. I believe that you too can do the same with every Potential within you.

This transformation happens effectively when you accept Jesus as your Lord and savior and begin to delight in His Word. He promises to give you the desires of your heart and everything that is necessary for you to live a fulfilling life. I believe that you should not only HEAR the Word of God but you should DO the Word of God. Hearing the Word of God gives you faith but faith without works is dead.

Each devotion has at least one lesson that can be learnt. Identify the lessons by answering the questions that follow each devotion and make your action plan and begin to take action. As you take these actions, the Lord will begin to transform your Po to Pro.

All scriptures quoted in the digestion are referenced in the additional food sources.

I declare that it will be unto you according to His Word. Every promise that God has made to you through His Word will be fulfilled and you will live a life of purpose. I declare that you will prosper and be in good health as your soul prospers, as you feed it with this **Spiritual Food**.

SPIRITUAL FOOD

VOLUME 1

Convert Your Potential To Product (PO to PRO)

Food Source: Psalms 27:10 NKJV

Food: *"When my father and my mother forsake me, Then the LORD will take care of me."*

Nutrient: God Will Take Care of You

Digestion: At age 18, I dropped out of University because they broke into my father's house and murdered his wife. He was accused and arrested for the murder but was acquitted a few years later. My sister's mother was left in charge of his business at the time and she told me that he had said that I should not get any more money from her and that I should go and seek a job. I was depressed, angry, I felt abandoned and betrayed but I prayed and God reminded me of this Psalm in our food today and it comforted me. Even though it turned out to be a lie I learned to trust in God to take care of me.

Few months later God blessed me with a job and I got back into University part time to do my degree in Construction Management. I was able to pay my tuition for the first year. I did very well that year so the second year I applied for scholarships and God favored me with them until I completed my degree 6 years later. He blessed me with a car and a house by the time I was 28 years old and a new job that was paying me over 10 times more than I was earning when I started working. After reflecting on His faithfulness towards me I had to surrender my life completely to Him in 2013.

Today if you will trust God and surrender your lives to Him, He will do even greater things for you. The bible says that He will supply all our needs according to His riches in glory if we seek Him first. *Eye has not seen, nor ear heard, nor have entered into the heart of man the things which God has prepared for those who love Him.* Have you been abandoned by those who are supposed to take care of you? God will take care of you if you just allow Him to and trust Him.

Grocery Shopping: Father I thank You that Your Word does not lie and that You take pleasure in taking care of us Your children if we obey You. Whatever the needs of Your children are today Lord, supply them I pray. Show us a sign of Your goodness today that we may testify and glorify You in Jesus' name I pray, amen.

Additional Food Sources: Philippians 4:19, Matthew 6:25-33, Psalm 37:4, 1 Corinthians 2:9

What setbacks have you experienced in your life?

_____
_____
_____
_____
_____
_____
_____
_____
_____
_____
_____

Do you believe that God can turn things around for you? Find a verse to encourage your faith, write it and meditate on it.

_____
_____
_____
_____
_____
_____
_____
_____
_____
_____

Day 2

Food Source: Jonah 1:12 NIV

Food: *"Pick me up and throw me into the sea," he replied, "and it will become calm. I know that it is my fault that this great storm has come upon you."*

Nutrient: Storm for Disobedience

Digestion: God wanted Jonah to go to Nineveh to warn the people about their wickedness but Jonah refused to do God's Will and decided to go his own way on a ship to Tarshish instead. So God sent a mighty, violent storm that would tear the ship apart. The mariners were afraid and began to cry out to their gods and lighten the loads of the ship. They even cast lots to figure out who caused the storm and it fell on Jonah. Jonah confessed that he was the cause of the storm because he had disobeyed God and fled from His Presence. In our food he told them to throw him overboard and after doing so the storm ceased from raging.

Some of us have been going through some storms in our lives, trial after trial and tribulation after tribulation and we can't understand why. Sometimes it is because of our disobedience to God and the fight we put up against His will and plans for our lives. You cannot win this battle! This storm will continue to rage in your life until

4

you accept God's Will for your life and become obedient.

After Jonah was thrown overboard, he was swallowed by a great fish and was in its belly for three days and three nights. He had to pray a prayer of repentance and conform to God's Will to be released from this prison that he was in and put an end to his trial. What storm have you been experiencing in your life? Could it be because of your disobedience? Surrender to God's Will and plans for your life today and end this storm of disobedience because obedience to God is more important than anything else in your life.

Grocery Shopping: Father help us to accept that Your will must be done on earth as it is in heaven. Help us to be obedient to Your plans and quit fighting the losing battle against Your will. As we conform to Your will, end the storms in our lives and restore us in Jesus' name I pray, amen.

Additional Food Sources: Jonah 1-2, Matthew 6:10, 1 Samuel 15:22, Romans 8:28-30

What storms have I been experiencing because of disobedience?

_____
_____
_____
_____
_____
_____
_____
_____
_____
_____
_____

What steps can I take to end my storms?

_____
_____
_____
_____
_____
_____
_____
_____
_____
_____
_____

Day 3

Food Source: Psalms 30:5 NKJV

Food: *"For His anger is but for a moment, His favor is for life; Weeping may endure for a night, But joy comes in the morning."*

Nutrient: He Will Make You Smile Again

Digestion: David made a terrible mistake and sinned against God by taking a census. It caused 70,000 people to die because God sent a plague on the land as a result. When the prophet Gad came to him he told him that he'd rather be at the mercy of God than of man because he knew God was Merciful. So David repented and God relented and restored his joy. God's discipline is not always pleasant but his anger does not last forever.

We all make mistakes, some detrimental but we have the power to change our situations by acknowledging them and correcting course. It may be a bad financial decision, a job that's sucking the life out of you, a bad relationship choice that is making you unhappy, you may be living in sin, whatever it is God is saying my favor is for a lifetime, I am a God of Judgment but also Love, Mercy and Forgiveness. I want to make you smile again.

Just like David repented and God relented and restored his joy, He is waiting for you to repent so that He can restore your joy and make you smile again. What sin do you need to repent of? All you have to do is confess it to God and repent. He promises to forgive you and He will not remind you of your sins and torment you with them but He will remember them no more. Do it today so that like David in our food you can say, "For His anger is but for a moment, His favor is for life; Weeping may endure for a night, But joy comes in the morning."

Grocery Shopping: Father we are thankful that You are merciful and Your desire is for us to live a happy and fulfilling life. Help us to repent of our sins and give up those things that are causing us to be unhappy so that we can experience Your mercy and joy and begin to smile again in Jesus' name I pray, amen.

Additional Food Sources: 2 Samuel 24:1-25, Psalm 51, Hebrews 8:12

What lessons did I learn from this message?

_____
_____
_____
_____
_____
_____
_____
_____
_____
_____
_____
_____

What are my action plans?

_____
_____
_____
_____
_____
_____
_____
_____
_____
_____
_____

Day 4

Food Source: Genesis 29:35 NKJV

Food: *"And she conceived again and bore a son, and said, "Now I will praise the LORD." Therefore she called his name Judah. Then she stopped bearing."*

Nutrient: Give God the Praise

Digestion: Jacob had fallen in love with Laban's daughter Rachel and agreed to work 7 years for her but he was deceived and given Leah as his wife because the tradition was that the firstborn had to be married first. So he had to work another 7 years for Rachel and ended up with two wives. When God saw that Leah was not loved He gave her children but made Rachel barren.

Leah was desperate to make Jacob love her. When she gave birth to her 1st son Reuben, she said now my husband will love me but that didn't happen. When she gave birth to her 2nd son she named him Simeon because she said God has heard I am unloved. The 3rd time she named her son Levi because she said Jacob must be attached to her because she has given him 3 sons. That didn't happen because it didn't change the fact that he LOVED RACHEL!

Finally she got it and when she had the 4th son she said "Now I will praise the Lord" and called him Judah. It is important to note that this is the

10

tribe King David and The King of kings, Jesus came from. Many of us like Leah waste our lives trying to win the love of people who will never love us regardless of what we do. We need to recognize how special we are. We are fearfully and wonderfully made, the apple of God's eyes, He sacrificed His son for us because He loves us. You have to love yourself before you can love others. It is time we start valuing ourselves the way God does and give God the praise for His Marvelous creation.

Grocery Shopping: Father, I thank You that before I was in my mother's womb You knew me and You made me special and with a purpose. Help me to find for myself the same value that You have placed on me. Help me to hold my head up knowing that I am special to You and start walking in my purpose in Jesus' name I pray, amen.

Additional Food Sources: Genesis 29, Psalm 139:14, John 3:16, Psalm 17:8, Jeremiah 1:5

What self-worth challenges have I been facing?

_____
_____
_____
_____
_____
_____
_____
_____
_____
_____
_____
_____
_____

What steps can I take to see myself the way God sees me?

_____
_____
_____
_____
_____
_____
_____
_____
_____
_____
_____

<u>Day 5</u>

Food Source: 2 Samuel 24:24 NIV

Food: *"But the king replied to Araunah, "No, I insist on paying you for it. I will not sacrifice to the Lord my God burnt offerings that cost me nothing." So David bought the threshing floor and the oxen and paid fifty shekels of silver for them."*

Nutrient: Give God Your Best

Digestion: After David had sinned against God and He sent the plague upon the land, the Prophet Gad told him to build an altar on the threshing floor of Araunah the Jebusite. So David went to Araunah to buy the threshing floor but Araunah insisted that the King should take it for free but David replied in our food, "No, I insist on paying you for it. I will not sacrifice to the Lord my God burnt offerings that cost me nothing."

I wish all of us would just take this page from David's book because God says those who honor Me I will honor and those who despise Me shall be lightly esteemed. Many of us probably would have gladly accepted this land and even say it is a blessing from God but not David. He is a man who knows how to honor God and give God his best therefore free was not an option. He was adamant to pay for his sacrifice.

Like David we should endeavor to give God our best. We should give Him the same quality and

13

quantity we expect to receive from Him. The bible says he who sows sparingly will also reap sparingly and God loves a cheerful giver. The bible also says: do not be deceived, God is not mocked; for whatever a man sows, that he will also reap. What is your sacrifice? No matter what it is, whether it is your money, your service or your time, give God your best! As you do, He will honor you!

Grocery Shopping: Father, I thank You that You always give me Your best because You are Omniscient. Help me to show You the same gratitude and give You my best in every area of my life knowing that You promised to give back to me a good measure, pressed down, shaken together and running over, in Jesus' name I pray, amen.

Additional Food Sources: 2 Samuel 24:25, 1 Samuels 2:30, Galatians 6:7, 2 Cor. 9:6-8, Luke 6:38

Have I been giving God the best of my time, service and money? Assess each area.

_____
_____
_____
_____
_____
_____
_____
_____
_____
_____
_____
_____

What steps can I take to improve my giving in my weak areas?

_____
_____
_____
_____
_____
_____
_____
_____
_____
_____

Day 6

Food Source: II Corinthians 9:10 NKJV

Food: *"Now may He who supplies seed to the sower, and bread for food, supply and multiply the seed you have sown and increase the fruits of your righteousness,"*

Nutrient: Release Your Blessings

Digestion: One day I went by a restaurant to purchase lunch. As I drove up, I saw a lady standing outside with her daughter who was crying. I was immediately moved with compassion so I wound down my car window and asked her what was wrong. She said that they were hungry and she had no money to buy food for them to eat. I was so saddened by her story and their tears. I gave her some money to go and get some food. She lifted the money to heaven and gave God thanks. I must have been the answer to her prayers. She thanked me and left for the supermarket. I prayed for God to change her situation and began to thank Him for His blessings on me in spite of my challenges because this lady opened my eyes.

Many of us complain and take for granted the blessings of God instead of being thankful. Not being cognizant of the fact that there are people out there like this lady who don't even know where their next meal will be coming from. We

16

should be thankful and be kind to those who are in need and sow into their lives. Our food today is saying that God will supply and also multiply the seed we have sown and increase the fruits of our righteousness. God has supplied you with seed but if you have not sown your seed then there will be no fruit to increase. Giving is a way to release your blessings. Few days after I gave this lady that money, I received an unexpected 6 figure cheque.

Society teaches us to save in order to get rich but the bible teaches us to give in order to be rich. Quite contrary but when you sow into the lives of those in need you activate God's promises and release your blessings. He multiplies your seed and increases the fruits of your righteousness. God is Faithful to His Word. Do you want to release your blessings? Obey God's Word and sow into the lives of the needy and watch Him release your blessings and multiply your seed.

Grocery Shopping: Father, thank You for Your blessings that we take for granted ever so often. There are so many around us who are suffering for different reasons. Open our bowels of compassion so that we can sow into their lives. As we obey, release our blessings and multiply our seeds in Jesus' name I pray, amen.

Additional Food Sources: Matthew 25:31-46, 2 Corinthians 9:6-15, Proverbs 3:27-28

Think of ways in which you can help the needy.

_____
_____
_____
_____
_____
_____
_____
_____
_____
_____

What are steps can you take to begin helping them today?

_____
_____
_____
_____
_____
_____
_____
_____
_____
_____

Day 7

Food Source: Proverbs 3:27 NIV

Food: *"Do not withhold good from those to whom it is due, when it is in your power to act."*

Nutrient: Do All the Good You Can

Digestion: One day I was on my way to work and I saw a man on the bypass whose car seemed to have broken down. There was a strong urge to stop and help that I could not shake. So I stopped and I found out that he had run out of gas and his kids were in the car, late for school. I took him to the gas station to get some gas and took him back to his car. I can't remember this man's face or his name but I never forgot the joy I felt.

Sometime after, I was driving from Clarendon in a hurry to get home to catch my landscaper when a goat ran out into the path of my car. I hit it and it died on the spot. The bumper of the car was torn off and other parts were also damaged. I don't know where these men came from to assist but I didn't even lift a finger. The parts that had fallen off were back in place, the dead goat was moved out of the road and I was back on my way in a few minutes. My aunt also gave me some money to replace the parts that were damaged.

I am not saying that the two stories are directly related but one thing I am sure about, when you do good to others it comes back to you. We will all have our day when we need the help of others and in the end, only kindness matters. Kindness is an expression of love and God wants us to love one another. There is also an unexplainable joy that doing good brings that no money can buy. If you have the world's goods and see your brother or sister in need and shut up your heart, how does the love of God abide in you?

Today ask the question, how can I help? You are God's hands in the earth so always look for ways in which you can help others. When it is in your power to do good for others never say no.

Grocery Shopping: Father, I thank You for Your infallible Word that covers every aspect of life and teaches us to live with each other. Help us to read Your Word daily so that we may know how to treat each other. Help us never to withhold good from each other. Help us to always be willing to help, not to be rewarded but to act in obedience to Your Word and to be an expression of Your love to others so that You may be glorified. In Jesus' name I pray, amen.

Additional Food Sources: Proverbs 3:28, 1 John 3:16-18, Mark 12:28-31, Hebrew 13:1-3, Luke 6:27-36

How did this message impact my life?

_____
_____
_____
_____
_____
_____
_____
_____
_____
_____
_____

How can I apply what was read to my life?

_____
_____
_____
_____
_____
_____
_____
_____
_____
_____

Day 8

Food Source: Matthew 6:34 NLT

Food: *"So don't worry about tomorrow, for tomorrow will bring its own worries. Today's trouble is enough for today."*

Nutrient: Stop Worrying

Digestion: I discovered one of the most interesting quotes when I read Dale Carnegie's book: **How to Stop Worrying and Start Living**. He said, *"Today is the Tomorrow You Worried about Yesterday."* In most cases, the things that we worried about yesterday never happen today. That is why our food is saying to us, stop worrying about tomorrow's trouble and only focus on today's trouble. We live our lives in distress and never experience the joy that we should because all we do is worry.

The fact is, worrying does not change situations, it only cause us to be sick and impede our ability to think and see simple solutions that God has been showing us. Most times the solution to our problems is right in front of us. Mr. Carnegie gives this practical solution to worrying; ask yourself and answer these 3 questions as they will help to solve most problems:

1. What is the problem?
2. What are the possible solutions to the problem?

22

3. What is the best solution to the problem? After you have answered number 3 you do it right away.

As Believers we should have faith and trust God to fulfill His promise and supply all our needs according to His riches in glory. Sometimes the reason we don't have is because we worry instead of asking. He says that whoever asks receives, those who seek will find and those who knock will have the door opened to them. We also need to look back at times when God came through for us and know that He is the same yesterday, today and forever more. What He did for you then He will do it for you again today. What are you worrying about today? God is saying that you need to stop worrying and trust Him. Let Him know what you need through prayer and supplication and stop worrying. Relax! Listen to His directions, ask, seek and knock. He will provide the solution.

Grocery Shopping: Father, You are faithful. Help us to increase our faith so that we will be able to obey Your Word and trust Your promises. Help us to put away anxiety, knowing that our future is in Your capable and mighty hands. Help us to be at peace so that we can hear and follow Your directions. Show us who to ask Lord, where to seek and which door to knock on for the solution to this problem today. As we obey You, cause us to testify of Your goodness and Your faithfulness in Jesus' name I pray, amen.

Additional Food Sources: Matthew 6:27, Hebrews 13:8 Philippians 4:6-7, James 4:2, Matthew 7:7-11

What can I take away from this reading?

_____
_____
_____
_____
_____
_____
_____
_____
_____
_____
_____
_____

What are my action plans?

_____
_____
_____
_____
_____
_____
_____

Day 9

Food Source: Matthew 19:26 NKJV

Food: *"But Jesus looked at them and said to them, "With men this is impossible, but with God all things are possible."*

Nutrient: All Things Are Possible

Digestion: Few years ago one of my friends called me in distress because a doctor had written off his hope of having a child and told him that it was impossible because his sperm count was low. Knowing the power of the God I serve and the authority He has given me to bind and loose I quickly rebuked that doctor's report. I reassured my friend that nothing is impossible for God and that He is the one who gives children. I told my friend that God's timing is the right timing and if He did it for Abraham and Sarah He can surely do it for him too.

Few years later his wife gave birth to a handsome little boy. I don't know what the doctor, the loan officer, your family, friends or your situation is telling you today but I want to tell you about the God I serve, who makes all things possible. He made the heaven and the earth in 6 days, He created man from clay, parted the mighty Red Sea, raised the dead after 4 days, shut the mouth of the lion, walked on water and fed 5,000 with 5 loaves and 2 fishes, just to list a few.

Relax my friend! Your situation is nothing! My God is Mightier than any situation you can present to Him! Today lift your faith and trust the Greatest Physician, Accountant, Chief Architect and Engineer. Man may be saying it is impossible but with God, ALL THINGS ARE POSSIBLE!

Grocery Shopping: Father, I embrace Your Omnipotence today knowing that with You all things are possible. Whatever the situation of Your children are today Lord, show up and show off! Remind them that nothing is impossible for You. I exalt You and thank You that it is already done in Jesus' name I pray, amen.

Additional Food Sources: Genesis 18:14, Job 42:1-2, Luke 1:37, Matthew 14:13-36

What impossible situation(s) am I facing?

_____
_____
_____
_____
_____
_____
_____
_____
_____
_____
_____
_____

What are my strategies to overcome these impossible situation(s)?

_____
_____
_____
_____
_____
_____
_____
_____
_____
_____
_____

Day 10

Food Source: Proverbs 22:6 NKJV

Food: *"Train up a child in the way he should go, And when he is old he will not depart from it."*

Nutrient: Train Them Up in the Fear of the Lord

Digestion: I thank God for blessing me with an awesome son, Zaire. He says some of the most amazing things at times. One day he said to me "Dad, I want to be a good boy for God." Another day we were going to church, before I discovered that it was my calling to become a Pastor. He said to me, "Dad, you look like a Pastor." I said thanks son, you look like a Deacon. He says "No! I am a Pastor too." His mantra is: I can do all things through Christ who strengthens me. One night he started having a stomach ache. Before he told anyone he began to pray and rebuke the pain. His grandmother heard him praying and joined him in prayer then gave him some tea for it.

As parents we should grow our children in the fear of the Lord. The fear of the Lord is the beginning of wisdom, and knowledge of the Holy One is understanding. Children will live what they learn. Teach your children by living the way of the Word, as this will make them want to live how you are living. Don't confuse them by saying one thing and living in a contrary manner. Even though some of us may not have had the best parental guide or even a good role model, let us change the cycle of 'do what I say not what I do' and become good examples for our children to follow.

A lot of parenting resources are available now, get them and make a concerted effort to be a better parent. Transformation in our society will only happen when we train the minds of our children correctly. Listen to them, learn from them, advise them, guide them, protect them, pray for them and love them. Let them say I want to be like my mom or dad. Be an example to your children and train them up the right way, in the fear of the Lord because they will not depart from it.

Grocery Shopping: Father, thank You for the gift of parenthood that You have blessed some of us with. Help us to appreciate and utilize this opportunity to develop brilliant, godly, loving men and women who will change the future of our society. Bless those who are ready but having challenges to reproduce. We rebuke the spirit of barrenness and we declare that they will be fruitful and multiply. Help us to be godly parents and role models that our children are proud to emulate in Jesus' name I pray, amen.

Additional Food Sources: Ephesians 6:4, 2 Timothy 3:15, Proverbs 9:10, 13:22, 17:6

How has this lesson taught me to train up my child?

_____

_____

_____

_____

_____

_____

_____

_____

_____

What can I do to change my mindset of parenting?

_____

_____

_____

_____

_____

_____

_____

_____

_____

Day 11

Food Source: Mark 11:23 NKJV

Food: *"For assuredly, I say to you, whoever says to this mountain, 'Be removed and be cast into the sea,' and does not doubt in his heart, but believes that those things he says will be done, he will have whatever he says."*

Nutrient: Your Faith Can Move Your Mountain

Digestion: Jesus was teaching me this lesson that He taught His disciples in this text when I was about 10 years old but I did not fully understand it until I became a Christian at age 28. At that time I was living with my grandparents and they had a big pear tree in the yard that produced some really nice pears. It was too big for me to climb. So I would check daily to see if any had fallen but the pears would not fall from the tree so I could have them to eat. One day I got so mad that I rebuked the tree, I said "I wish tomorrow when I come around here I see you flat on the ground!"

The next day as I opened my eyes, remembering my Words I got up and hurried to check the pear tree. To my surprise it was laying on the ground with pears all around! Amazingly, it never died because the roots were still anchored in the ground. It lay on the ground for years bearing. I

31

never forgot that day and what I had accomplished by just speaking and believing.

When I finally understood this text, I realized I had done it that day, I spoke to that tree and it obeyed me because I exercised my faith. My life has never been the same since activating that faith and the power that lay dormant in me. I have seen God move so many mountains (obstacles) in my life because I believe and exercise my faith. What is your mountain today? God is saying if you would just activate your faith and believe without doubting you can tell your mountain to move and it shall move!

Grocery Shopping: Father, I thank You for the power that You have given us. Not many of us realize it but I pray that You will help us to open our eyes today and help us to activate our faith, see it and utilize it to move every mountain in our lives. Mountains of: financial struggle, sickness, failure, destiny prevention, sin, doubt, hurt, hate, unforgiveness and barrenness I command you to move in Jesus' name I pray, amen.

Additional Food Sources: Mark 11:12-24, James 1:5-8, Matthew 7:7, Hebrews 11:1&6

What are some of the faith blockers in my life?

_____

_____

_____

_____

_____

_____

_____

_____

_____

_____

_____

What steps can I take to stir my faith?

_____

_____

_____

_____

_____

_____

_____

_____

_____

_____

Day 12

Food Source: Proverbs 18:24 NIV

Food: *"One who has unreliable friends soon comes to ruin, but there is a friend who sticks closer than a brother."*

Nutrient: My Closest Friend

Digestion: Today I just want to introduce someone to my closest friend Jesus. He has been closer than a brother to me even when I wanted to do my own thing and was caught in sin. When I was a child He placed the dream to become a Pastor in my heart and now He has shown me that it is my destiny. I love His presence so much that I got locked up in church one night but I was never afraid. I just found my way to the altar and slept on the cushions until it was morning and I was safe.

During the absence of my parents He gave me a guardian, Aunty Queen who loved me like I was her own. When I was about 12 years old the devil tried to kill me by an accident but God protected me and I came out with only a few stitches. He tried again when I was 20 years old but this time Jesus made me unconscious and took me to a safe place for a few hours. I only remember the remarks, "Only Jesus saved you". He has always taken care of me, He never fails me. I surrendered to Him and now I am walking in my destiny and getting even closer to Him daily and now my life is a testimony.

Most of you know Him but some of you refuse to surrender to Him and obey Him. Here is a friend who died for you because He loves you. He wants to be your:

C - Comforter

L - Lord

O - Oxygen

S - Saviour

E - Everything

S - Shepherd

T - Target, then

F - Favor you

R - Respond to you

I - Interact with you

E - Elevate you

N - Navigate for you,

D - Dwell with you.

Will you give him that chance today?

Grocery Shopping: Father I thank You for Your desire to be my closest friend. Help me to surrender to You, learn to trust You and make You my closest friend today in Jesus' name I pray, amen.

Additional Food Sources: John 15:13-17, James 4:4-10

What steps can I take to make Him my closest friend?

_____

_____

_____

_____

_____

_____

_____

_____

_____

_____

_____

_____

Day 13

Food Source: Genesis 50:19-20 NIV

Food*: "But Joseph said to them, "Don't be afraid. Am I in the place of God? You intended to harm me, but God intended it for good to accomplish what is now being done, the saving of many lives."*

Nutrient: He Is Using It for Your Good

Digestion: Joseph's brothers hated him because he was his father's favorite and he made him a coat of many colours. Then God showed him his destiny in two dreams that were interpreted to mean that his parents and brothers would bow down to him. He was rebuked by his father and hated even more by his brothers who wanted to kill him but God rescued him and he was sold into slavery in Egypt instead. While serving as a slave in Egypt he was promoted by his master Potiphar to ruler of his house because God's favor was upon him.

The devil would not have it that way so he used Potiphar's wife to accuse him of rape because he refused to grant her wish of sleeping with her. He would not sin against his God so he ran from her leaving his cloak. He was put into prison but God's favor was with him even in prison and he was given authority over his inmates. During this time, he discovered the ability to interpret dreams and he interpreted the dreams of Pharaoh's cup bearer and baker who were restored and hanged respectively as interpreted. 2 years later this ability promoted him to Prime Minister, gave him a wife and all the wealth and power he could desire.

Like Joseph, some of us have enemies who are trying to kill our dreams. But God is working behind the scenes and using what was meant for your demise to train you and to push you into your destiny to help others. Stay faithful to God and trust Him because He has the blueprint for your life and He is navigating you to your destiny. The journey to your reigning may take a while. Do not be disheartened, you will become Prime Minister of your Egypt and those that meant you harm will be the very instrument that will be used to honor you because of the favor of God that is on your life. God will work all disappointments and setbacks for your good.

Grocery Shopping: Father I thank You for the plans that You have for my life. Even though the devil is fighting against them You are working things out for my good. Help me to trust You and remain faithful to You in Jesus' name I pray, amen.

Additional Food Sources: Genesis 37:3-11, 26-28, 39:1-4, 7-23, 40:6-23, 41:37-46, 45:1-9

What are some of the things that God is using in my life to work for His good?

_____

_____

_____

_____

_____

_____

_____

_____

_____

_____

_____

How can I use these lessons to advance my life?

_____

_____

_____

_____

_____

_____

_____

_____

_____

_____

Day 14

Food Source: Proverbs 17:22 NIV

Food: *"A cheerful heart is good medicine, but a crushed spirit dries up the bones."*

Nutrient: Keep Your Heart Cheerful

Digestion: A good way to facilitate healing of the body is to keep your heart happy. Depression takes away your strength and causes your body to even resist medical treatment. So we should make a concerted effort to keep our hearts happy by scheduling regular time away from things that cause us to feel stressed and unhappy. Is there a game, television program or other activity that takes your mind away from everything and relaxes you? Include it in your schedule to help you cope with the stresses of life.

During my free time, one of my favorite games to play with my friends is ludo which we call "ludi" in Jamaica. This is one of the most amazing games to play. It totally takes my mind off everything because of the attention that is required. It is a game that also helps to build my faith and reassures me of the power that lies within the tongue. I find it so amusing when I speak to the dices before me or my opponents throw, guess what is going to be thrown and see it pop up on the dices. This game gives me and my friends a lot of joy and helps us to keep our hearts cheerful.

Our food is reminding us to keep our hearts cheerful because it is good medicine. If that is the case, shouldn't you make an extra effort to keep your heart cheerful? Do something fun today my friend, keep your heart cheerful. Why would you want to entertain a crushed spirit if it dries up your bones? Save some money on doctor bills. That's what you will be able to do when you keep your heart cheerful.

Grocery Shopping: Father I thank You for this reminder to keep our hearts cheerful because it is good medicine, another way of saying stop worrying! Give us Your peace and help us to find happiness in our lives and rid ourselves of the things that cause depression. Help us to get close to You and stay close to You because in Your presence there is fullness of joy in Jesus' name I pray, amen.

Additional Food Sources: Psalm 16, Proverbs 12:25, 15:13-15

What are the things that are causing my heart not to be cheerful?

_____
_____
_____
_____
_____
_____
_____
_____
_____
_____
_____

What steps can I take to regain a cheerful heart?

_____
_____
_____
_____
_____
_____
_____
_____
_____
_____
_____
_____
_____
_____

Day 15

Food Source: Proverbs 19:14 NIV

Food: *"Houses and wealth are inherited from parents, but a prudent wife is from the Lord."*

Nutrient: **Allow God to Help Choose Your Partner "Part 1"**

Digestion: God takes interest in all aspects of our lives that is why the scripture says in ALL your ways acknowledge Him and He will direct thy path. Choosing a wife or husband that is not God's Will for your life can be detrimental to your happiness and purpose. We must therefore allow God to be a part of the selection process and exercise extreme caution. Our food says parents can give us an inheritance but a prudent (wise, sensible in action and thought) wife is from the Lord. Therefore we should fast and pray to God for the right person for us and seek wise counsel.

He knew us before we were formed in our mother's womb, and He is All-Knowing. Therefore this qualifies Him to be the Best Judge of Character. One of the main reasons marriages fail is because of incompatibility. We sometimes choose a partner that it is impossible to agree on anything with and two cannot walk unless they agree. This is the same reason the bible advises us not to be unequally yoked with unbelievers, those who are not saved or do not share the same religious beliefs.

When we get married there should be harmony which gives access the "power of two". The bible says one shall chase 1,000 but two shall put 10,000 to flight. Solomon says two is better than one because one may be overpowered but two can defend themselves. It is also important to note that the devil is actively involved in this process with the aim of joining incompatible people together to cause hate, hurt, adultery, destruction of families, unhappiness, diversion from purpose and ultimately divorce. Therefore, exercise extreme caution and allow God to help choose your partner!

Grocery Shopping: Father I thank You that Your aim is for me to be equipped to fulfill my purpose. It is therefore important for me to have the right partner to spend the rest of my life with. Help me not to be deceived by the devil and trust only my emotions but allow Your Holy Spirit to help me to select my partner. Direct me to the right person in Jesus' name I pray, amen.

Additional Food Sources: Amos 3:3, 2 Corinthians 6:14, Proverbs 3:5-6, Deuteronomy 32:30, Ecclesiastes 4:9-12

What are the strategies that I learnt from this lesson?

_____
_____
_____
_____
_____
_____
_____
_____
_____
_____

How can I practically put what I learnt into practice?

_____
_____
_____
_____
_____
_____
_____
_____
_____

Day 16

Food Source: Matthew 19:6 NKJV

Food: *"So then, they are no longer two but one flesh. Therefore what God has joined together, let not man separate."*

Nutrient: **Allow God to Help Choose Your Partner "Part 2"**

Digestion: If God has helped to choose your partner, then nothing should be able to separate you especially if you abide by the Word of God, forgive each other, be faithful to each other and love according to 1 Corinthians 13. Love never fails and it is able to withstand all things. It is never self-seeking because the two become one flesh. What affects one person also affects the other person therefore you both should be striving to please each other and make each other happy by doing God's Will.

As I indicated in **"Part 1"** the devil also joins people together. Usually this union is to oppose God's Will and plan for your life. Usually there is no harmony so the couples function as two separate entities which cause arguments about almost anything and everything. There is constant unhappiness and ultimately hatred. There are cases where people joined by the devil come into contact with Jesus and change because they now get in alignment with God's Will. A man

45

testified that he used to abuse his wife until he got saved and Jesus changed him into a loving husband. If this kind of transformation does not take place, these people should not remain together because two cannot walk unless they agree.

What God has joined together always involve harmony and the main purpose of this union is to fulfill God's Purpose for your life. No man is able to separate this union as seen in our food. Therefore, attraction should be first spiritual then emotional and physical instead of the contrary which is usually the case because our motive is the fulfillment of sexual desires rather than God's Purpose. The person that God joins you with will most likely be your soulmate, the person He has created for you to help you to attain your full potential and accomplish His purpose for your life. Allow God to help choose your partner because when He does you will be happy and inseparable.

Grocery Shopping: Father I acknowledge that the devil is cunning and he is always in opposition to Your will and plans for my life but You are Greater and Your will must be done. If I have been his victim I ask that You release me from the devil's control today and help me to get in alignment with Your will and plan for my life.

Lord, please connect me with my soulmate in Jesus' name I pray, amen.

Additional Food Sources: 1 Corinthians 13:3-8

What lessons did I learn from this message?

_____

_____

_____

_____

_____

_____

_____

_____

_____

_____

_____

What are my action plans?

_____

_____

_____

_____

_____

_____

_____

_____

Day 17

Food Source: Matthew 19:9 NKJV

Food: *"And I say to you, whoever divorces his wife, except for sexual immorality, and marries another, commits adultery; and whoever marries her who is divorced commits adultery."*

Nutrient: **Allow God to Help Choose Your Partner "Part 3"**

Digestion: The final reason you need to allow God to help choose your partner is that marriage is a serious covenant and God does not like divorce. I have only found two circumstances in the bible where divorce and remarriage is permitted. Firstly, when there is sexual immorality as seen in our food. This is when your partner is unfaithful. Secondly, if you were married before you became saved and your partner is not a believer and the unbelieving partner choses to get a divorce. If you divorce for any other reason, then you should not remarry.

I do believe however that if God did not join you together and the devil did; if you are faithful to God and diligently seek Him for a solution He will make a way of escape since it was never His will. God is a God of Judgment but He is also a God of Mercy and Forgiveness. When you get in alignment with His will and He joins you with

48

your soulmate however, His Word always takes precedence.

It is therefore paramount that God is involved in the selection process and you exercise extreme caution. Nobody wants to spend the rest of their lives alone and it is not God's Will for us to be alone or live an unhappy and unfulfilled life. It is therefore also important to get pre and post marital counselling, invest the necessary time and effort required to know and understand your partner and always allow God to be at the center of everything. There are a lot of resources available about relationships and marriage, get them and use them. I recommend the movie: *"War Room"* and the books: *"Five Love Languages by Gary Chapman* and *His Needs, Her Needs by Willard F. Harley, Jr."*

Grocery Shopping: Father, even though marriage seems impossible with man I am thankful that with You all things are possible. Bless me with the right partner, love, happiness and the oneness that You desire. Help me to put You first in my relationship so that You can fight my battles and sustain my relationship to endure any storm in Jesus' name I pray, amen.

Additional Food Sources: Matthew 5: 31-32, Mark 10:1-12, 1 Corinthians 7:10-16

What lessons did I learn from this message?

_____
_____
_____
_____
_____
_____
_____
_____
_____
_____
_____
_____

What are my action plans?

_____
_____
_____
_____
_____
_____
_____
_____
_____
_____
_____

Day 18

Food Source: Daniel 6:22 NKJV

Food: *"God sent His angel and shut the lions' mouths, so that they have not hurt me, because I was found innocent before Him; and also, O king, I have done no wrong before you."*

Nutrient: God Will Shut the Mouth of Your Lion

Digestion: Few years ago I was deceived by the devil and made what would have been the biggest mistake of my life. I got married to the wrong woman. I was a man most miserable. When I realized what was happening I cried out to God in fasting and prayer and He heard my cry and gave me prophetic instructions to separate from her as it was not His will for my life, a story too long for this devotional but one that I will share in another book someday God's willing.

During an altercation with her she told me, "Do not wake a sleeping lion." I told her that she cannot do me anything because when God is fighting your battle no man can defeat you. Few days later I went to fasting service at Worship and Faith International Fellowship. That day Minister Kimola Brown-Lowe prophesied to me and said "God says to tell you to make your decision and I will shut the mouth of the Lion...!" 3 months later she moved out of my house and gave me a signed statement saying that she will not take me to court or fight me for my house or make any other claims from me. Few weeks prior to that, she was adamant that she wanted half of the equity of the house. I had told her to get her lawyer and make her claim because my freedom, peace and God's Will meant more to me.

Today, I don't know what Lion you are facing whether it is an abusive spouse, enemies, debt, financial struggle, lack of jobs, barrenness, loneliness or fight from coworkers but if you let yourself be found innocent and righteous before God, He will shut the mouth of that Lion so that it cannot hurt you. He did it for Daniel and He did it for me, today He can do it for you too. Daniel God surely will deliver and shut the mouth of your lion!

Grocery Shopping: Father I thank You that You take pleasure in shutting the mouths of lions, people who think they are too mighty and situations that overwhelm us. Today I put my lion before You, (tell Him your lion) shut its mouth for me I pray in Jesus Mighty name, amen!

Additional Food Sources: Psalm 91, 2 Timothy 4:17-18, Hebrews 11:33

What lions am I facing?

_____

_____

_____

_____

_____

_____

_____

_____

_____

_____

Write what God instructs you to do.

_____

_____

_____

_____

_____

_____

_____

_____

_____

Day 19

Food Source: Proverbs 15:1 NIV

Food: *"A gentle answer turns away wrath, but a harsh Word stirs up anger."*

Nutrient: Give a Gentle Answer

Digestion: One day, a friend of mine sent me a message that I found to be very offensive and disrespectful. In my response, I ended up adding fuel to the fire. I was expressing my lack of appreciation for her disrespectful behavior for a situation I had nothing to do with. I was being spewed on because my brother had helped to create this frustrating situation. It even got to the point where she said, "you can delete me and block me, I don't care."

Thank God for the fruit of the Spirit: love, peace, patience, gentleness and self-control. I would have lost a friend but God kept me in perfect peace with today's food and allowed me to be a part of the solution instead of the problem. I realized that she was just venting and she needed my help. So instead of blowing off more steam I said, "It is ok my friend, go ahead and vent. We will address your manners when you calm down but how can I help?" That response caused the situation to take a U turn, I was able to calm her down and offer assistance to solve her problem. She ended up telling me, "That is why I love you so much." I ended up thanking her for today's Spiritual Food.

The bible is infallible and if we live by it and the Holy Spirit's guidance we will never go wrong. Our nations would be a better place if we just apply the principles in the bible and love one another. Napoleon Hill said, *"Never say something hurtful to someone because it will hurt you 10 times more."* The bible says that we are to be quick to listen, slow to speak and slow to become angry because the anger of man does not produce the righteousness that God desires. It also says that *"Starting a quarrel is like opening a floodgate, so stop before a dispute breaks out."* Does a fireman take fire to put out a fire? Today, never fight fire with fire but use water instead. Cool off before addressing a heated situation or try to be patient and give a gentle answer. A gentle answer will turn away wrath but harsh Words only stirs up anger and it will make a bad situation even worse.

Grocery Shopping: Father I thank You for Your Holy Spirit that dwells in us when we accept You as Lord and Savior. He keeps us in perfect peace because of His fruit, love. Help us to accept You and have this experience today. Help us to be quick to listen, slow to speak and slow to anger. Help us to give a gentle answer in Jesus' name I pray, amen.

Additional Food Sources: Galatians 5:22-23, James 1:19-20, Proverbs 17:14

What lessons did I learn from this message?

_____

_____

_____

_____

_____

_____

_____

_____

_____

_____

What steps can I take to ensure that the fruit of the Spirit is evident at all times in my life?

_____

_____

_____

_____

_____

_____

_____

_____

_____

_____

Day 20

Food Source: 1 Peter 5:8 NLT

Food: *"Stay alert! Watch out for your great enemy, the devil. He prowls around like a roaring lion, looking for someone to devour."*

Nutrient: Know How the Devil Works "Part 1"

Digestion: When you buy a new phone or device, in order to be able to use it effectively you have to read the manual or watch a video in order to know how it works if you are not tech savvy as some of us are. It is the same thing with an enemy. In order to fight your enemy, the devil effectively, you must understand how he works, his strengths and weaknesses. Our food says he prowls around like a roaring lion looking for someone to devour. His job is to rob, kill and destroy. In order not to fall prey, we must learn how he works.

Two of the most profound books I have read are **Outwitting the Devil by Napoleon Hill** and **Unmasking the Devil by John Ramirez**. These books expose the devil and the tools he uses to keep us in sin, devour us and ultimately win our souls. I believe that these books should be read along with the bible as they give a very detailed description of how the devil works. I believe that God used these authors to provide us with this critical information for such a time as this.

Outwitting the Devil was written in 1938 but was never published until 2011 because of fear. I was lead to this book during a time of fasting. It helped me to realize what the devil had been doing in my life and as a result I was able to break free, stay alert and now walking in my destiny. In order to stay alert one must first be aware. So over the next few days I will share some biblical principles also outlined in this book that will help us to understand how the devil works.

I learnt at school from I was a child growing up that "Knowledge is Power" but it was only about 2 years ago that I discovered that a critical part of that statement is missing! The correct statement is: "knowledge is power when it is applied" Think about it! Even though I am willing to share my knowledge with you, if you do not apply it to your situation, you will not access its power. Take the time and learn how the devil works my friend so that you will be able to outwit him.

Grocery Shopping: Father You are the Most High God, You are All-Knowing, All-Powerful and You are everywhere. There is none like You! You have already conquered the devil and we are guaranteed that same victory today. Help us to open our minds to learn how he works and apply that knowledge so that we have the power to fight him, defeat him and stay alert in Jesus' name I pray, amen.

Additional Food Sources: John 10:10, 12:31, 2 Corinthians 4:3-6, 11:14-15, Luke 10:18-20, 2 Timothy 1:7

What lessons did I learn from this message?

_____
_____
_____
_____
_____
_____
_____
_____
_____
_____
_____

What are my action plans?

_____
_____
_____
_____
_____
_____
_____
_____
_____

Day 21

Food Source: 2 Corinthians 4:4 NLT

Food: *"Satan, who is the god of this world, has blinded the minds of those who don't believe. They are unable to see the glorious light of the Good News. They don't understand this message about the glory of Christ, who is the exact likeness of God."*

Nutrient: Know How the Devil Works "Part 2"

Digestion: Paul says in our food that Satan (the Devil) is the god of this world and interestingly in this book (Outwitting the Devil: an interview between Napoleon Hill and the Devil), the devil says he controls 98% of the people of this world while his opposition (God) only controls 2% because he is better at marketing. That is, enticing us by our desires. James 1:13-14 says that God cannot be tempted by evil nor does he tempt anyone but we are tempted when we are drawn away (caused to "drift") by our own desires and enticed.

The devil has no physical body; he is not a beast with forked tongue and a spiked tail but consists of negative energy. His favorite place to occupy is the minds of people. This is why Paul says in Ephesians 6:12 NLT *"For we are not fighting against flesh-and-blood enemies, but against evil rulers and authorities of the unseen world, against mighty powers in this dark world, and against evil spirits in the heavenly places."*

God controls positive thoughts (good) and the devil controls negative thoughts (evil). He controls the minds of people by occupying the unused space of our brains. He puts negative thoughts in our minds and uses it to occupy this space. So whenever we have negative thoughts we are giving the devil control of our mind. This is why Paul in Philippians 4:8NIV is saying *"Finally, brothers and sisters, whatever is true, whatever is noble, whatever is right, whatever is pure, whatever is lovely, whatever is admirable—if anything is excellent or praiseworthy—think about such things."* He is telling us to always keep our thoughts positive so that the devil cannot control our minds.

Grocery Shopping: Father I thank You for exposing the work of the devil. I pray that You will release Your people from his control. I rebuke and bind up every negative thought today and loose positive thoughts in the minds of your people. I rebuke you devil! Flee from God's people now in the Mighty name of Jesus, amen.

Additional Food Sources: James 1:13-16, Ephesians 6:10-18, Philippians 4:8

What negative thoughts have I been entertaining?

_____
_____
_____
_____
_____
_____
_____
_____
_____
_____
_____
_____

What steps can I take to get rid of these negative thoughts and keep my thoughts positive?

_____
_____
_____
_____
_____
_____
_____
_____
_____

Day 22

Food Source: II Timothy 1:7 NKJV

Food: *"For God has not given us a spirit of fear, but of power and of love and of a sound mind."*

Nutrient: Know How the Devil Works "Part 3"

Digestion: In the book: **Outwitting the Devil by Napoleon Hill**, the Devil states that one of his cleverest devices for controlling our mind is fear. Paul states that God has not given us a spirit of fear so this must be from the devil and therefore concurs with this claim. He says he plants these seeds of fear in the minds of people and as they germinate and grow through use, he controls the space they occupy. Therefore another way to eliminate the Devil's control of our mind is to conquer and eliminate all forms fear and this is crucial for believers since it is not of God and the Devil's cleverest device.

The **six most effective fears** are: the **fear of poverty, criticism, ill health, loss of love, old age** and **death**. He says that the ones that serve him most are poverty and death. At one point or another during life he tightens his grip on us through one or both of these fears. He accomplishes this by making people believe that he is standing just beyond the entrance gate of the next life, waiting to claim them after death for eternal punishment. Of Course He cannot punish anyone, except in that person's own mind, through some form of fear. Fearing something which does not exist is just as useful to him as fear of that which does exist. All forms of fear extend the space he occupies in the human mind.

I hope I have whet your appetite enough for you to want to know how your enemy the Devil works and now you are eager to get these two books and read them for yourself. The second book, **Unmasking the Devil** was written by **John Ramirez** who was a victim and became a devil worshipper for 25 years but found Jesus and was saved. He shares his interesting testimony in another book called **Out of the Devils Cauldron.** He confirms some of these devices and illustrates biblically, how the devil works and gives strategies to also overcome the devil in this book, **Unmasking the Devil**. Jesus is more powerful than the devil and all of his devices and He can help you to overcome him but lack of knowledge will surely cause you to perish. Get them today and claim your victory through Jesus Christ.

Grocery Shopping: Father I thank You for making us aware of some of the Devil's cleverest devices to control our minds. No longer will your people perish because of lack of knowledge. We rebuke and bind up his demons and devices in the name of Jesus. We pray for wisdom to outwit him and the grace to embrace the fact that You have not given us a spirit of fear but of power and of love and of a sound mind. Help us to overcome the devil in our lives and fulfil Your purpose in Jesus' name I pray, amen.

Additional Food Sources: Proverbs 1:7, John 14:27, Romans 8:15, 1 John 4:17-18, Hosea 4:6, 2 Corinthians 10:3-6

What tools has the devil been using against me?

_____
_____
_____
_____
_____
_____
_____
_____
_____

List steps to overcome and to outwit the devil

_____
_____
_____
_____
_____
_____
_____

Day 23

Food Source: 2 Corinthians 12:9 NLT

Food: *"Each time he said, "My Grace is all you need. My power works best in weakness." So now I am glad to boast about my weaknesses, so that the power of Christ can work through me."*

Nutrient: **Strength in Your Weakness**

Digestion: During my Bachelor of Science in Construction Management degree program at the University of Technology, Jamaica I went blank in a final exam. That day I spent 4 hours in the library with my friends preparing for the exam that was scheduled for 1pm. When I was packing up to get to the exam my friends asked me where I was going and I told them to the exam. They laughed and told me that the exam was at 5pm. I had printed the schedule early, it was changed and I was never notified. Anyway I spent another 3 hours or so studying, a total of about 7 hours.

When I got into the exam and they instructed us to begin I was looking through the paper and to my amazement all of those 7 hours were pointless because nothing I had studied was on the paper and I was clueless. 30 minutes later, when it was ok to leave the exam room, about half of my classmates had left. I had failed an exam before, which cost me J$30,000 and an additional year to redo. Failure was not an option for me so I began to pray. I said, "Lord I need Your wisdom now because I have nothing." I was in that exam until they said stop writing, Words just kept flowing. That night I had a terrible headache but when the results came I got an A-.

As our food says God's power works best when we are weak. When we realize that without Him we are nothing and we begin to trust Him, that is when His power becomes most effective and we can achieve the impossible. Today, whatever that impossible situation is, acknowledge your weakness and allow Jesus to take control. Let Him be your strength in your weakness; allow His power to work through you.

Grocery Shopping: Father I thank You that when I am weak, strength is always available in You. What seems impossible to me is a simple thing for You because You specialize in the impossible and with You all things are possible. Help me to trust You and allow Your power to work through me today in Jesus' name I pray, amen.

Additional Food Sources: Proverbs 3:5-6, Philippians 4:13, 2 Corinthians 12:10, Isaiah 40:29-31

What are my areas of weakness?

_____

_____

_____

_____

_____

_____

_____

_____

_____

_____

_____

What steps can I take to allow God to strengthen
me in these areas?

_____

_____

_____

_____

_____

_____

_____

_____

_____

_____

_____

Day 24

Food Source: Proverbs 21:5 NLT

Food: *"Good planning and hard work lead to prosperity, but hasty shortcuts lead to poverty."*

Nutrient: **Plan and Work Hard for Prosperity**

Digestion: I got my first job when I was 19 years old and I have been working ever since. Shortly after I started working, I created and wrote down my list of goals that I wanted to achieve by the time I got to the age of 30. The list included: a house, a car, a masters, marriage and getting saved. I normally did a New Year's resolution at the beginning of each year and make a list of all I wanted to achieve for that particular year. I would monitor my progress throughout the year to see what I had achieved and update the list as necessary, striking off achieved goals and adding new goals as the desires came.

I usually write out Philippians 4:13 "I can do all things through Christ who strengthens me" at the bottom of the list and pray about it. I believed that anything my mind conceived I could achieve it. The other thing I did was work hard. I maintained a spirit of excellence and did my best in everything I did. I was working and going to school and I was never delinquent. At a staff meeting my boss once told the others, "If you are going to work and go to school, do it like Clatin. I

69

don't know how he does it but you need to find out."

I achieved most of those goals before I got to the age of 30. Today I embrace those principles because they worked for me and I encourage you to try them today. What are your goals? Write them down, determine how to achieve them and work hard towards them daily until they are achieved. You will be prosperous because as our food says, good planning and hard work leads to prosperity! If you seek to get rich quickly without applying principles you definitely will become poor.

Grocery Shopping: Father I thank You for the dreams You have placed in my heart. Help me to realize today that I can achieve them all if I apply the principles of proper planning and hard work. Help me not to use hasty shortcuts or be discouraged by failure but see it as an opportunity to change my strategy and keep trying until I succeed. Thank You for my achievements and those You have in store for me in Jesus' name I pray, amen.

Additional Food Sources: Proverbs 10:4, 19:15, 12:24, 13:4

List your goals and strategies to achieve them.

_____

_____

_____

_____

_____

_____

_____

_____

_____

_____

_____

_____

Set time lines for achieving each goal.

_____

_____

_____

_____

_____

_____

_____

_____

_____

_____

_____

Day 25

Food Source: Colossians 3:13 NLT

Food: *"Make allowance for each other's faults, and forgive anyone who offends you. Remember, the Lord forgave you, so you must forgive others."*

Nutrient: **Forgive Them Today**

Digestion: Forgiveness is never the easiest thing to do especially when the person has hurt you badly. But the reality is we all make mistakes and we all will need forgiveness at some point in our lives, if not from that person from someone else or from God. Jesus said if we forgive others then our Heavenly Father will also forgive us of our sins but if we refuse to forgive others then He will not forgive us of our sins. When we are living in sin it is not easy for us to appreciate this fact.

After I got saved forgiveness became easier for me. When I reflected on all the sins I have committed and the fact that God loved me so much that He sent his son to die for me and He is willing to forgive me of my sins if I just confess them to Him and repent. Since I will need His forgiveness then I will always forgive others too. Have you ever done something very bad when you were a child and you felt like your parents were going to punish you severely? Do you remember the relief you felt that time when they said, "it is ok but don't let it happen again?" Or can you relate with a similar situation?

Forgiveness helps you to heal and allows you to be at peace with yourself and others and it allows God to hear your prayers. Today think about that person you have not forgiven. Remember that time when you received forgiveness. You are not perfect so you will need forgiveness again. Don't allow that one person or event to ruin the rest of your life. If we want God to forgive us we must forgive others too. Do yourself a favor and forgive them today.

Grocery Shopping: Father I thank You for Your Grace today. Thank You for the many times You have forgiven me. Help me to extend forgiveness to (say the person's name) today. What he/she did really hurt but I forgive him/her today. Thank You for setting my heart free and help me to always forgive my offenders and experience Your peace in Jesus' name I pray, amen.

Additional Food Sources: Matthew 6:12-15, Mark 11:25-26

Ask the Holy Spirit to reveal to you the person (s) that you need to forgive.

_____
_____
_____
_____
_____
_____
_____
_____
_____
_____
_____
_____

Take a decisive action to call, text and speak to person(s) that the Holy Spirit revealed to you.

_____
_____
_____
_____
_____
_____
_____
_____
_____
_____

Day 26

Food Source: Proverbs 19:5 NKJV

Food*:* *"A false witness will not go unpunished, And he who speaks lies will not escape."*

Nutrient: **Always Speak the Truth**

Digestion: When I was a child growing up I was told the story of the boy who cried wolf! The little boy, when he was on his way home from school would cry, "Wolf! Wolf! Wolf!" Everyone would run to his rescue but only to be aggravated by his lies and had to go back home probably upset. One day the wolf finally showed up. He cried, "Wolf! Wolf! Wolf!" But nobody came to his rescue because they thought maybe it was another prank.

Telling lies is not a good thing even if it is being done for fun as in this little boy's case. It is one of the six things listed by Solomon that God hates. When you tell a lie you will always have to tell another one to cover up the one you told before and therefore you create a never ending cycle. I have heard the saying every liar is a thief. I don't agree but that's the stigma attached to it. Lies destroy trust. If you tell a person a lie, even if you are forgiven it may cause them to be cautious and as a result unable to fully trust you.

Today, always speak the truth because it is said that the truth will set you free. Honesty is the best policy! Lying lips are an abomination to the Lord and in our food he says that the liar will not escape punishment. When you speak the truth you build integrity and trust. The truth is easier to forgive and the truth will rescue you in times of trouble. Always speak the truth.

Grocery Shopping: Father I thank You that You are a God who delights in the truth. Help me to delight in the truth and walk in Your truth daily. Lord if it is a curse that I have inherited I declare that curse broken and I declare that from today I will always speak the truth in Jesus' name I pray, amen.

Additional Food Sources: Proverbs 6:16-19, Proverbs 12:22, Proverbs 11:20, Proverbs 21:28

Areas in my life that I am not always truthful.

_____
_____
_____
_____
_____
_____
_____
_____
_____
_____
_____
_____
_____

Steps that I can take to always be truthful no matter what.

_____
_____
_____
_____
_____
_____
_____
_____
_____
_____
_____
_____

Day 27

Food Source: Galatians 5:14 NIV

Food: *"For the entire law is fulfilled in keeping this one command: "Love your neighbor as yourself."*

Nutrient: Love Is the Solution

Digestion: I don't know much about history and slavery because I didn't love reading in high school. One day I was discussing racism with a friend and I realized that most of it stems from slavery, the history of what the "white man" did to the "black man". I concluded that I am glad I did not corrupt my mind with such history. I am glad that I lived my life by the Word of God and I have never seen white man or black man in the bible. God says love one another! Why? Love covers a multitude of sins and the entire law is fulfilled in this commandment, love your neighbor as yourself.

Knowledge can be good but also harmful if it is not supported by wisdom. I do appreciate what our heroes have done to allow us this freedom and being rooted and grounded in God's Word I will make myself knowledgeable someday but it is time we move past this. Paul says one thing I do is forgetting what is behind and looking forward to what lies ahead. We cannot rewrite the past. We are not in slavery physically anymore; let us not allow ourselves to be in slavery mentally because of history.

I am not saying we should be naive to its existence. I am saying we can break the cycle by not planting this negative seed in our children because a child's mind is pure until it becomes corrupted by knowledge. Teach them to love one another as themselves because love is the solution. We are all Gods people, He made us all and He just wants us to love one another. Our heart is what matters to Him. Let us liberate ourselves through Jesus and fill the hearts of our children with love by loving one another because love is the solution.

Grocery Shopping: Father I thank You for Your demonstration of Your love for us through Your son Jesus. Help us to obey this commandment to love one another today because it is the solution to the problems in our society: racism, hatred, the violence, wars, poverty and so many others. Lead us to You today and teach us to love because we won't know love until we find it in You, in Jesus' name I pray, amen.

Additional Food Sources: Matthew 22:36-40, Philippians 3:13, James 2:8, Romans 13:8-10, Matthew 7:12

Do you remember having any feelings of hatred towards anyone because of what you have read or have been taught?

_____
_____
_____
_____
_____
_____
_____
_____
_____
_____

What steps can you take to eradicate these feelings of hatred and live in love?

_____
_____
_____
_____
_____
_____
_____
_____
_____
_____

Day 28

Food Source: John 2:15 NLT

Food: *"Jesus made a whip from some ropes and chased them all out of the Temple. He drove out the sheep and cattle, scattered the money changers' coins over the floor, and turned over their tables."*

Nutrient: Anger Can Be Used Positively

Digestion: Anger combined with passion can be a very powerful emotion and can be used to yield positive results if we exercise self-control and utilize it properly. This is why the bible does not forbid anger, in fact Paul says be angry but do not sin, do not let the sun go down on your anger. In our food Jesus got angry at those who were selling in His Father's house. He made a whip and chased them out of the temple, scattered the coins, overturned the tables and warned them to stop turning His Father's house into a market place. He put an end to this ungodly and irreverent act.

A few years ago I was listening to one of my favorite teachers, Pastor Chip Ingram on his program *Living on the Edge*. He shared a story of how he used his anger positively. He was in the laundromat and he saw a lady slam her child's arm in the dryer because she was angry for whatever reason. He got so angry that he walked up to her and said, "if you lay another hand on that child I will knock your lights out and I am a pastor." He said it would have been the first time he would have hit a lady and he would not have felt guilty about it.

He could not sleep the night. All he could think about was the child and the abuse and the fact that he needed to do something about it. This passion and anger lead him to form an organization to help children who are being abused. So you see, anger can be used to bring about positive results if we exercise self-control and utilize it properly. What positive change can you use your anger to make today? Let us use this powerful emotion to change the bad things we see happening around us: the abuse, the violence, the corruption, the hatred, injustice, crime, racism and other ungodly practices.

Grocery Shopping: Father we know that the anger of man does not produce the righteousness that You desire if self-control is not exercised. Help us to realize that it is a powerful emotion that can also be used to change the bad things happening around us. Teach us self-control and how to use this emotion positively today in Jesus' name I pray, amen.

Additional Food Sources: John 2:13-16, Ephesians 4:26-27, Psalm 4:4

What lessons did I learn from this message?

_____
_____
_____
_____
_____
_____
_____
_____
_____
_____
_____
_____

Steps to turn my negative anger into positive anger.

_____
_____
_____
_____
_____
_____
_____
_____
_____
_____

Day 29

Food Source: Isaiah 59:2 NKJV

Food: *"But your iniquities have separated you from your God; And your sins have hidden His face from you, So that He will not hear.*

Nutrient: Sin Blocks Prayer

Digestion: To effectively communicate with God and have a good relationship with Him we must be without sin. Therefore we need to confess our sins to God on a daily basis and repent of them because we sin even in our very thoughts. The bible says that we all have sinned and come short of the glory of God. From our food we see that sin causes God to hide His face from us and also prevents Him from hearing our prayers. Also our iniquities cause us to be separated from God. God is Holy and we must be holy in order to be close to Him and to get His attention when we pray.

There is only one sin that is unforgivable and that is blasphemy of the Holy Spirit. No other sin is too big for God to forgive because He promises to forgive us once we confess and repent. He does not haunt us with our sins but throws them into the sea of forgetfulness and remembers them no more. So there is no need to be burdened by them. Repent, forgive yourself and move on. Sin blocks prayer so don't entertain them, get rid of them today.

When David had committed adultery with Bathsheba, he repented thoroughly and wrote Psalm 51 as a result. He asked God not to cast him away from His presence nor take His Holy Spirit from him. David acknowledged the importance of God's presence, His Holy Spirit dwelling and communicating with him and so should we. Let us evaluate our lives daily and consistently acknowledge our sins, confess them to God, repent and seek His forgiveness. Sin causes God to hide His face from us and it blocks our prayer. Do you want your prayers to be blocked? Certainly not! Let us therefore be holy before our Heavenly Father.

Grocery Shopping: Father I thank You that Your Grace is sufficient for any condition and any sin. Lord I confess all known and unknown sins to You today. Wash me in Your blood, cleanse me and turn Your face back to me and answer my prayers in Jesus' name I pray, amen.

Additional Food Sources: Romans 3:23-26, 5:19-20, Galatians 5:19-21, Mark 3:28-30, Hebrews 8:12, Psalm 51

What sins have I been entertaining that may be blocking my prayers?

_____
_____
_____
_____
_____
_____
_____
_____
_____
_____
_____

What steps can I take to get rid of these sins in my life?

_____
_____
_____
_____
_____
_____
_____
_____
_____
_____

Day 30

Food Source: Isaiah 53:5 NKJV

Food: *But He was wounded for our transgressions, He was bruised for our iniquities; The chastisement for our peace was upon Him, And by His stripes we are healed.*

Nutrient: God's Healing Power, Still Active!

Digestion: A Few years ago my aunt was diagnosed with multiple fibroids. The doctor told her that she had to do a surgery to remove her womb because the largest one was sitting on her spine. This caused her to have constant back pain. She was adamant in her stance not to do a surgery. She told the doctor that she is leaving this earth with all the body parts that God gave her. She lifted her faith by not taking her medications but prayed for divine healing from God. When she did the scan a few months later, the doctor reported that all the fibroids were gone except one which had been reduced in size from 3cm to 1.5cm.

I want to remind someone struggling with a health condition that God's healing power is still active today and you can be healed by His stripes! All you have to do is lift your faith like my aunt and receive your healing. God does not show partiality but in every nation whoever fears Him and walks in righteousness is accepted by Him.

So the same thing He did for the woman with the issue of blood, blind Bartimaeus and my aunt, He will do for you if you have faith. So lift your faith and believe God for your healing today.

I emphasize faith because I have observed from scriptures that this is what will move God to act in your situation. James says that the one who doubts should not expect anything from God. In most if not all cases, Jesus told those who got healed that it was their faith that healed them. I believe therefore that faith is your doctor's fee. Just as you can't see a doctor without his fee, you can't go to God for healing without faith. Jesus is the same yesterday, today and forever therefore that same healing power is still available to you today. Use your faith to access it now.

Grocery Shopping: Father, I stand on Your Word that by Your stripes I am healed. I lift my faith to You today knowing that You are the greatest physician and You are still working miracles. (Put your hand on your head and declare) I am healed and made whole; I command every sickness or disease to leave my body right Now in the Mighty name of Jesus, amen.

Additional Food Sources: Acts 10:34-35, Luke 8:43-48, Mark 10:46-52, 16: 17-18, James 5:14-16, Hebrews 13:8

What sickness do I need to access His healing power for?

_____

_____

_____

_____

_____

_____

_____

_____

_____

_____

What are steps am I going to take to gain access?

_____

_____

_____

_____

_____

_____

_____

Day 31

Food Source: Matthew 12:31 NKJV

Food: *Therefore I say to you, every sin and blasphemy will be forgiven men, but the blasphemy against the Spirit will not be forgiven men.*

Nutrient: Try Saving, Stop Condemning!

Digestion: I was greatly disturbed by a video that my friend showed me of a Pastor voicing his ungodly opinion about the gay club shooting in Orlando, Florida on June 12, 2016. It is just sad that some of us in our anger are quick to forget God's Word and His crucifixion. We judge and condemn others even though we know that we all have sinned and fallen short of His glory.

Even though we disapprove of the sin of homosexuals and it is an abomination to God, we should never condemn the individuals because He forbids us to do so since His Grace is sufficient to save all. Our food tells us that only blasphemy against the Holy Spirit is unforgivable! You can never be too deep in sin that you cannot be redeemed. Paul was murdering the Disciples of Jesus when he was Saul but God converted him and made him one of the greatest Apostles and New Testament authors.

God does not want anyone to perish that is why He sent His son. Let us stop defeating the purpose

90

of Jesus' crucifixion! Let us stop judging and condemning! Let us try to save sinners! If you have not made an attempt to tell a person about Jesus then you are not even in a position to even try judging them! Our job is to share the gospel and allow the Holy Spirit to bring conviction that will lead to salvation. If we fail, let God be their judge, do not condemn them!

Grocery Shopping: Father we thank You for sending Your Son to die for us. Help us never to forget what He did for us on Calvary and the Grace it gives us. Help us as believers to leave all judgment to You and play our role to spread the gospel and rescue sinners. Help those of us who are sinners to receive your Grace and repent of our sins in Jesus' name I pray, amen.

Additional Food Sources: James 1:20, Leviticus 18:22, Matthew 7:1-3, Luke 6:37, Romans 5:8, 2 Timothy 3:16-17

What lessons did I learn from this message?

_____
_____
_____
_____
_____
_____
_____
_____
_____
_____
_____
_____

What steps can I take to share the gospel with others?

_____
_____
_____
_____
_____
_____
_____
_____
_____
_____

Day 32

Food Source: 1 Samuel 18:1 NIV

Food: *"After David had finished talking with Saul, Jonathan became one in spirit with David, and he loved him as himself."*

Nutrient: Appreciate Your Jonathan

Digestion: Jonathan was the son of Saul, the first king of Israel. In our food, we see that after David had killed Goliath Jonathan became one in spirit with David and he loved him as himself. Because David was successful in battle, the women would cheer when he came back home, shouting that Saul killed a thousand but David ten thousands. As a result of this, Saul despised David and an evil spirit came upon Saul and he tried to kill David. So for many years David had to be running from him.

Because Jonathan loved David, he did everything to protect him. At first he did not believe that his father would try to kill David. When he found out that it was true, he pleaded for David but his father was so angry that he tried to kill him. Jonathan honored his covenant with David nevertheless and helped him to escape his Father. Jonathan had died when David finally became King, he blessed Jonathan's son Mephibosheth for Jonathan's sake and the love he showed him.

I have been blessed with a few people in my life like Jonathan, people who love me unconditionally and will do everything in their power to help me. Do you have any Jonathan in your life? If you have one or more Jonathan in your life, you are blessed and you should appreciate them. They are God's gift to you to help you to get to your destiny and fulfill your purpose here on earth. Are you appreciating your Jonathan? If you have not already started, begin to show appreciation to the Jonathans in your life today.

Grocery Shopping: Father I thank You for Your promise never to leave us nor forsake us. In keeping with this promise You have placed some Jonathans in our lives to help us get to our destiny and fulfill our purpose. Lord we thank You for our Jonathans, our destiny helpers. Lord, help us to connect with our Jonathans today. Help us to appreciate them because they are Your gift to us to help us fulfill our purpose in Jesus' name I pray, amen.

Additional Food Sources: 1 Samuel 20:16-17, 2 Samuel 1:17-27, 9:1-13

What lessons did I learn from this message?

_____
_____
_____
_____
_____
_____
_____
_____
_____
_____
_____
_____

What are my action plans?

_____
_____
_____
_____
_____
_____
_____
_____
_____
_____
_____
_____

Day 33

Food Source: Psalm 34:19 NIV

Food: *"The righteous person may have many troubles, but the Lord delivers him from them all;"*

Nutrient: Deliverance from All Your Troubles!

Digestion: Few years ago my aunt bought a car in my name to do some business and assist me with travelling to school. One night my brother was dropping his friend and another guy home and met in a terrible accident in which the guy died. It turned out that the insurance rejected my claims because the insurance did not cover his age and I was not made aware of it. The other party in the accident was claiming, the family of the dead guy, even the friend that he was dropping home made a claim for injury without us knowing. It was the most stressful time of my life, I felt like the world was caving in on me and all I could do was pray.

What is your trouble today? Are you feeling like there is no solution and this is the end of the road? Our food says the righteous person may have many troubles, but the Lord delivers him from them all. Let me tell you how God delivered me out of that situation. God sent a Good Samaritan that works with the insurance company to assist. The insurance decided to

96

honor the claim of all the other parties. I ended up getting an ex gratia payment, even though it was not enough to fix the car I was thankful because it helped to pay the loan for a few months.

I thought my brother had the car in the garage repairing but it turned out that the car was scrapped with only the shell remaining. I defaulted on the loan and the bank came for what was left of the car. They sent a bailiff to claim the remaining balance on the loan but after a few months he disappeared. When I called him he said don't make any more payment because usually the loan is written off at this stage. God did it for me; today He can do it for you! No matter what the trouble is God will deliver you if you are found righteous in His sight. All you have to do is take it to Him in prayer, be patient and trust Him. He will deliver you from all your troubles!

Grocery Shopping: Father when I think of Your goodness and what You have done for me my soul cries out Hallelujah! Daniel God I exalt Your Excellence today! Lord I don't know the trouble of the person reading this message but You know it all Lord! Just like You did for me time and time again, do it for Your children today! Show them a sign of Your goodness that they may glorify You in Jesus' name I pray, amen.

Additional Food Sources: Psalm 34, Proverb 24:16, Job 5:19

What lessons did I learn from this message?

_____
_____
_____
_____
_____
_____
_____
_____
_____
_____
_____

What are my action plans?

_____
_____
_____
_____
_____
_____
_____
_____
_____

Day 34

Food Source: Psalm 46:10 NIV

Food: *"He says, "Be still, and know that I am God; I will be exalted among the nations, I will be exalted in the earth."*

Nutrient: Just Be Still

Digestion: My son's mom had to take an emergency trip to Jamaica because her mom was sick and the doctors in St Kitts did not know exactly what was wrong with her. When she saw the doctor, he recommended a brain scan because he suspected that the condition was vertigo. However, when she did a brain scan the results showed that it was not the case and everything was fine. When she was ready to go back home, she asked me to book the flight for her to leave the Wednesday. At first, the ticket prices were very high. I told her not to worry but just to wait because they will go down. The Monday when I checked they were down by US$200. So I tried to book her flight online but the airline rejected the card and there was no connecting flight available. I told her to relax, she will go home the Wednesday. I called the airline and got them to hold the reservation but after several attempts the card was just being rejected. Now she was very worried but I just kept saying, "relax, you will go home Wednesday."

The next time that I went online, the connecting flight became available so I booked it. We had to go to the airline's office to make payment for the other connecting flight but the card was still being rejected. We went to the ATM to get the cash and at first we could not get any cash and the bank said nothing was wrong with the card. Now she started to sweat because she was really worried but I kept saying, "relax you will go home Wednesday". After several attempts we got the cash and booked her flight. I said, "you see, I told you, you will go home Wednesday!" When you know the God that you serve and His power, all you have to do is be still when the storms are raging. Nothing is impossible for Him, some situations are out of our control and those are the ones He specializes in but He needs your trust, He just wants you to be still and know that He is God. Today my friend, be still and know that He is God! Leave that situation to Him.

Grocery Shopping: Father you are God all by Yourself, there is no storm that can rock your boat because the earth is Yours and everything in it, You made it. Help us to be still today and know that You are God. Help us to trust You, give us your peace to relax knowing that You are still in control and if You be for us then nothing and no one can be against us. Father show up in our situations today and cause us to glorify You, testify of Your goodness and increase in faith in Jesus' name I pray, amen.

Additional Food Sources: Psalm 46

What situation is causing me to worry or lose hope today?

_____
_____
_____
_____
_____
_____
_____
_____
_____

What can I do to relax and be still? Write some verses to help.

_____
_____
_____
_____
_____
_____
_____
_____
_____

Day 35

Food Source: Hebrews 12:6 NLT

Food: *"For the LORD disciplines those he loves, and he punishes each one he accepts as his child."*

Nutrient: God Disciplines Those He Loves

Digestion: Few years ago I made the worst decision of my life and married the wrong woman. Before I went through with it my best friend warned me. Even my mother and my father warned me and did not come to the wedding because they did not support my decision. I was stubborn because I heard what I wanted to hear and convinced myself it was from God and ignored their advice.

I paid dearly! I was a man most miserable, I faced financial difficulties, I was separated from my son and I was so unhappy. I cried out to God and He heard me and gave me the message more clearly: "Separate yourself from them; I have warned you before. God is a God of Judgment, God is a God of mercy, God is a God of forgiveness. Exposure, exposure, exposure is coming!" This time I listened! The exposures came and as I moved in obedience, my happiness was restored and the financial burden was relieved.

One day after writing my devotion and reflecting I was in tears. I asked God, what did I do to deserve this Grace, this mercy, and this favor? Today He is saying you are my child, I love you, I want what is best for you and I will discipline you until you learn. Your trials may be because of disobedience, God is disciplining you not because He hates you but because you are His child and He loves you. Evaluate your life today; ask yourself, "have I been disobeying God?" Take heed today because God disciplines and punishes those He loves and accept as His children!

Grocery Shopping: God, thank You for being a good good Father. Thank You for never giving up on me but disciplining me because You love me. I surrender to Your will today. Teach me to hear Your voice more clearly and obey You, in Jesus' name I pray, amen.

Additional Food Sources: Hebrews 12:3-11, Proverbs 3:11-12

What lessons did I learn from this message?

_____
_____
_____
_____
_____
_____
_____
_____
_____
_____
_____
_____
_____
_____

What are my action plans?

_____
_____
_____
_____
_____
_____
_____
_____
_____
_____
_____
_____
_____

Day 36

Food Source: Matthew 24:35 NKJV

Food: *"Heaven and earth will pass away, but My Words will by no means pass away."*

Nutrient: The Word of God Will Stand Forever

Digestion: Some time ago I got a very interesting message which highlights some changes that have been made to the NIV, NLT, ESV and other versions of the bible app on mobile devices. Usually I ignore these messages but I was astonished when I actually checked the bible app and see that the verses have actually been deleted! So the devil has found another way to rob us and has launched the attack.

He is trying to take away the power from the Word of God by removing 64,545 Words and over 40 complete verses. If he has removed these Words and verses it simply means that they contain power that is causing serious damage to his kingdom and therefore we should closely examine them. The Word of God is infallible and our food states that even though heaven and earth will pass away the Word of God will not pass away, it will stand forever! So this will be another failed attempt by the devil but unfortunately he will deceive many.

So what do we need to do to fight back?

- Do what David says and hide the Word of God in our hearts (study and memorize it)
- Stop being enslaved by these devices since it is the plan of the devil to use them to distract and manipulate us.
- Get hard copies of the bible before these changes because they cannot be altered.
- See article: https://www.jesus-is-lord.com/nivdelet.htm

Grocery Shopping: Father I thank You that Your Word cannot fail and will stand forever despite the Devil's attempt to rob us of its power. Help us not to be deceived but to hide Your Word in our hearts and use it to defeat the devil. He has attacked the gospel of Jesus Christ because Jesus is the way, the truth and the life but every knee will bow and every tongue confess that Jesus Christ is Lord. Devil you are already defeated in Jesus' name I pray, amen.

Additional Food Sources: John 10:10, Psalm 119:11, John 14:6, Philippians 2:10-11

What lessons did I learn from this message?

_____
_____
_____
_____
_____
_____
_____
_____
_____
_____
_____
_____

What are my action plans?

_____
_____
_____
_____
_____
_____
_____
_____
_____
_____
_____

Day 37

Food Source: Proverbs 18:10 NKJV

Food: *"The name of the LORD is a strong tower; the righteous run to it and are safe."*

Nutrient: **Run into the Strong Tower**

Digestion: Today there are so many things happening around us, fulfillment of end time prophecies such as earthquakes in diverse places, nations rising against nations, men being lovers of themselves, unholy, unloving, unforgiving, without self-control, brutal, lovers of pleasure rather than lovers of God. The bible says that we are not to be troubled because these things must come to pass. The end is not yet but it is the beginning of sorrow.

Let us stop acting blind, let us find the strong tower today and run into it. The name of the LORD is that strong tower. Jesus is the way the truth and the life, no man can come to the Father but through Him. Let us repent and walk after righteousness because only the righteous can run into the strong tower today and be safe. If you are living in sin today repent! If you are saved and not living righteous, repent! If you are righteous, share the good news of Jesus Christ with the unsaved today. Hold their hand and pull them into the strong tower. Let us all try to run into the strong tower so that we can be safe.

Grocery Shopping: Father You said that heaven and earth shall pass away before Your Word fails. Help us to recognize that the end is near and Your Word is being fulfilled. Help us to seek You while You may be found, call upon You while You are near, repent and walk after righteousness so that we can run into Your strong tower and be safe in Jesus' name I pray, amen.

Additional Food Sources: 2 Timothy 3:1-9, Matthew 24:4-14, John 14:6, Isaiah 55:6-8

What lessons did I learn from this message?

_____
_____
_____
_____
_____
_____
_____
_____
_____
_____
_____

What are my action plans?

_____
_____
_____
_____
_____
_____
_____
_____
_____
_____
_____

Day 38

Food Source: Colossians 3:23-24 NKJV

Food: *"And whatever you do, do it heartily, as to the Lord and not to men, knowing that from the Lord you will receive the reward of the inheritance; for you serve the Lord Christ."*

Nutrient: Work as unto God

Digestion: I got my first job at the National Works Agency in August 2004 and spent about 9 years there. For about 6 years I was being underpaid. My boss tried everything in his power to get me an increase. I completed a certificate in Construction Engineering, Diploma then a Bachelor of Science Degree in Construction Management and not even an increment to my salary. I worked diligently and efficiently nevertheless, earning the respect of my coworkers and my boss.

Eventually we were promoted to the Directorate of Regional Implementation and Special Projects. A program came on stream through which my boss was able to promote me from level 2 to 5 in 2010. 3 years later when he decided to start his own company, he considered me for a position in his company. I did not hesitate to accept the offer since I was already trying to leave and it would be a better opportunity for me.

I now understand the principle that I was applying back then. Napoleon Hill says offer greater service than that which you are paid to do and eventually you will be paid more than the service you offer. Our food says whatever you do; you should do it heartily as unto God and not men. Whether it is your job, serving at church or voluntary service in your community, do it to the best of your ability at all times to honor God regardless of the situation. Many of us have jobs and work with people that discourage, frustrate and do not compensate us properly. If you apply this principle however and work as unto God, He will reward you in due season because those who honor God He will also honor.

Grocery Shopping: Father I thank You that You see our hard work and You promise to reward us if we do whatever we do as unto You and not to men. I declare that your people will be promoted. I declare that they will become entrepreneurs. Rebuke the devourer from the reward of their hard work. Release their compensation and blessings as they honor You, in Jesus' name I pray, amen.

Additional Food Sources: Ecclesiastes 9:10, Colossians 3:17, Psalm 90:17, Proverbs 12:24, 14:23

Am I being diligent in what I do to honor God?

_____
_____
_____
_____
_____
_____
_____
_____
_____
_____
_____
_____

What steps can I take to function more diligently and to honor God?

_____
_____
_____
_____
_____
_____
_____
_____
_____
_____
_____

Day 39

Food Source: Psalms 90:12 NKJV

Food: *"So teach us to number our days that we may gain a heart of wisdom."*

Nutrient: Use Your Time Wisely

Digestion: Time is your greatest asset. It is the only thing which can be shaped into whatever material things you want but time waits on no man. Once it is gone you cannot reclaim it. Therefore it is important to learn to manage your time so that none of it is wasted. This Psalm was written by Moses. In the prior verses he establishes that our days are 70 to 80 years and we do not know when we will be cut off from this earth. In our food he was therefore praying for God to teach him to use his time wisely and today we need to do the same.

One of the things that I did over the years and later realized that it was my tool for never being delinquent while working and going to school was a To do list. Before I started my work day I would sit down, think about all the tasks I had to complete and make a list in order of priority. Discipline is also important. Never procrastinate. Complete each task and move to the next immediately. Skip those that cannot be completed or taking too long because of the mood you may be in. Do easier or more fun tasks then go back to that task. Add incomplete tasks to the top of tomorrow's list if nothing of greater importance comes up.

Anything practiced over time becomes a habit. Are you using your time wisely? Time management is a good thing to learn, practice and make a habit if you want to be successful in life and fulfill your purpose. Find time management tools and use them. Start using your time wisely today.

Grocery Shopping: Father I thank You for the time that You have given me. Help me to use it wisely so that none of it is wasted. Most importantly, help me to discover my purpose and use my time to fulfil it so that You may be glorified and at the end of my time here on earth I will hear the Words "well done thou good and faithful servant" in Jesus' name I pray, amen.

Additional Food Sources: Psalm 90:4-12, Ephesians 5:15-17, Colossians 4:5, Ecclesiastes 3:1-8

How have I been wasting time?

_____
_____
_____
_____
_____
_____
_____
_____
_____
_____
_____
_____

What steps can I take to better manage my time?

_____
_____
_____
_____
_____
_____
_____
_____
_____
_____
_____

Day 40

Food Source: Matthew 4:19-20 NKJV

Food: *"Then He said to them, "Follow Me, and I will make you fishers of men." They immediately left their nets and followed Him."*

Nutrient: **Make Yourself Available**

Digestion: Jesus was selecting his disciples in this text. He was walking on the Sea of Galilee and He saw two fishermen casting their nets, Simon called Peter and his brother Andrew. Our food says He said to them "Follow Me and I will make you fishers of men." The response of these men is very interesting and should be noted. They did not ask any questions, maybe they did not understand the statement He made, maybe they did not know the man, they did not know how they would survive and they did not know where they were going. But they immediately left their nets and followed Him.

This is the response Jesus wants from us today. He wants us to become like Simon Peter and Andrew and just make ourselves available. What happens when we make ourselves available to Him? Jesus is able to use us. He is able to change us, He is able to use us to do great things, He is able to use us to lead others to Him, He is able to give us power, He is able to restore us when we falter, He is able to use us to build a church, He is able to use us to guide others.

These are some of the things that Simon Peter did as a result of making himself available to Jesus. Jesus changed his name from Simon to Peter, Peter made the lame man walk, Peter walked on water, Peter caused many to be saved, Peter caused many to be filled with the Holy Spirit, Peter denied Jesus three times but Jesus restored him and used him to lead the apostles and start the early church. Today Jesus wants to use you to do greater things than these but you have to first make yourself available.

Grocery Shopping: Father, I know that You have a purpose for my life. Whatever my challenge is today, preventing me from availing myself to Your will I ask that You help me to overcome such challenges and help me to make myself available to you so that you can use me to do the works that You did and greater than those as promised in Jesus' name I pray, amen.

Additional Food Sources: John 1:42, Acts 2:1-4, Acts 2:41, Acts 3:1-9, Matthew 14:26-29, Matthew 16:18, Luke 22:54-62, John 14:12

Have I been making myself available?

_____
_____
_____
_____
_____
_____
_____
_____
_____
_____
_____

What steps can I take to be more available?

_____
_____
_____
_____
_____
_____
_____
_____
_____
_____
_____

Day 41

Food Source: Matthew 25:45 NIV

Food: *"He will reply, 'Truly I tell you, whatever you did not do for one of the least of these, you did not do for me."*

Nutrient: Be a Sheep

Digestion: Our food comes from the text that explains the separation of the saints that will take place when Jesus returns and the respective reward they will receive. We will be separated as a shepherd divides his sheep (righteous) from the goats (unrighteous). We will be judged based on our deeds. In this life we will come upon people who are in need; in need of food, drink, clothes, shelter, visit etc. God has blessed us to cater to the needs of these people.

The sheep will cater to these needs because they will love the shepherd and understand that whatever they do for those in need they are doing for Him. The reward will be the kingdom of heaven prepared for them. The goats on the other hand do not love the shepherd and as a result will not cater to the need of His people. Their reward will be everlasting punishment in the fire prepared for the devil and his angels.

Today let us strive to be a sheep. Sheep follows the shepherd because they love Him. The love we must have is an unfailing love like that which He

120

has for us. A Love that looks past offense, discouragement, faults, circumstances, feelings, qualification, deeds and all other negative things and still caters to the needs of others because we love Jesus and we are doing it for Him. Be a Sheep!

Grocery Shopping: Father you are the good shepherd, the greatest teacher and giver of love. You loved us so much You died for us even in our sin. Help me to love You and reflect this love to everyone that crosses my path. Help me to be a sheep and cater to the needs of Your people today with unfailing love in Jesus' name I pray, amen.

Additional Food Sources: Matthew 25:31-46

In what ways have I been functioning as a goat?

_____
_____
_____
_____
_____
_____
_____
_____
_____
_____
_____
_____
_____

What steps can I take to be more like a sheep?

_____
_____
_____
_____
_____
_____
_____
_____
_____
_____
_____
_____
_____

Day 42

Food Source: Psalms 119:105 NKJV

Food: *"Your Word is a lamp to my feet And a light to my path."*

Nutrient: Get 20/20 Vision

Digestion: A lamp is a device that produces light. Light is the agent that stimulates sight and makes things visible. So the Word produces light for our feet, which is the tool for walking/ running. The Word increases our ability to see and causes us to see things that are normally hidden from us as we walk or run. It means that without the Word you are like a blind man who cannot see the things around him while walking.

Let us not be like a blind man. Spend time in the Word of God. Some people naturally have a passion for the Word of God like me, while for some it is a challenge. Ask God for a passion for His Word. When you have a passion for the Word you will want to read it every day and when you start reading the Word you will be able to say thank God I was blind but now I see.

When you are reading the bible it is best to read an entire book in order to fully understand what the author is saying. So read a chapter or more a day until the book is completed then move to the next book. One of the best things I have ever done was to enroll in Preaching 101 at the Courtney

McLean School of Ministry. It took my passion for the Word to a different dimension and gave birth to my spiritual food. You can find this passion too. Start reading the Word of God and receive your sight. Get 20/20 vision by reading your bible daily.

Grocery Shopping: Father I thank You for enlightening my darkness. I do not want to be a blind man anymore but I want to have 20/20 vision. Help me to develop a passion for Your Word so that I will read it daily so it will be a lamp to my feet and a light to my path. In Jesus' name I pray, amen.

Additional Food Sources: Proverbs 6:23, Psalm 1:2-3, Psalm 119

Do I spend enough time reading the bible? If not, why?

_____
_____
_____
_____
_____
_____
_____
_____
_____
_____

What steps can I take to increase my passion and spend more time in the Word?

_____
_____
_____
_____
_____
_____
_____
_____
_____
_____
_____

Day 43

Food Source: Psalms 133:1 NKJV

Food: *"Behold, how good and how pleasant it is For brethren to dwell together in unity!"*

Nutrient: Power of Unity

Digestion: One of our core values at Worship and Faith International Fellowship is unity. For an entire week we experienced an awesome shift in the atmosphere because we decided to unite and meet as men. Lives were transformed and homes are being impacted and eventually this nation will be changed.

The Lord loves when we come together and unite. In our food the Psalmist uses an exclamation mark to express this strong emotion that results from brethren dwelling together in unity. In verse 2 of the Psalm he compares this to precious oil poured upon the head running down on the beard and running down is repeated to show its importance. When we unite to do anything pertaining to God, He shows up and His Powerful anointing flows from the leader down to everyone present.

It is indeed good and pleasant when we dwell together in unity. Today let us practice unity in our homes, in our communities, in our schools, in our churches and in our nation and experience the powerful anointing of God. God wants to do

126

something awesome in our nation but He requires us to unite first. Let us unite and experience the power of unity from God today.

Grocery Shopping: Father I thank You for the move that You are making in this season. I pray that You will infect this entire nation with the spirit of unity. I declare unity in our homes, in our families, in our schools, in our churches and in our communities and in our nation today in Jesus' name I pray, amen.

Additional Food Sources: Psalm 133, Matthew 18:20, Acts 2:1-4, Genesis 11:1-9

What have I been doing to foster unity in my surroundings?

_____
_____
_____
_____
_____
_____
_____
_____
_____
_____
_____

What further steps can I take to help more people to unite?

_____
_____
_____
_____
_____
_____
_____
_____
_____
_____
_____

Day 44

Food Source: II Kings 20:5 NKJV

Food: *"Return and tell Hezekiah the leader of My people, 'Thus says the LORD, the God of David your father: "I have heard your prayer, I have seen your tears; surely I will heal you. On the third day you shall go up to the house of the LORD."*

Nutrient: Prayer Can Change God's Verdict

Digestion: Hezekiah, the son of Ahaz and Abi became the King of Judah at the age of 25 and reigned for 29 years in Jerusalem. In the 14th year of his reign King Hezekiah became sick to the point of death and the Lord sent the prophet Isaiah to tell him to set his house in order because he was going to die. When he heard this he prayed to God and reminded Him that he walked before Him in truth, with a loyal heart and did what was good in His sight and wept bitterly.

Before Isaiah had gone out in the middle of the court the Lord sent him back to Hezekiah with a different verdict. He told him that he had heard his prayer and seen his tears and he will heal him on the third day as he went up to the house of the Lord. God gave him 15 more years and delivered him and the city from the King of Assyria. It is important to note the five ingredients that caused God to change His verdict:

1. He walked in truth

2. He had a loyal heart
3. He did what was good in God's sight
4. He prayed
5. He wept bitterly.

This is a strategy to be emulated. We need to walk in truth, with a loyal heart, doing what is good in God's sight and when we have sinned we weep to the Lord in prayer. Then we can be confident when we pray knowing that He will have mercy on us and answer our prayers. Today let us emulate Hezekiah and pray without ceasing for our destiny, our family and relatives, our churches, our leaders, for one another and our nations because prayer can change God's verdict!

Grocery Shopping: Father I thank You that You are a Merciful God. I thank You that every day new mercies I see. Help me to walk in truth, with a heart that is loyal to You and doing what is good in your sight. Help me to pray fervent, effectual and remorseful prayers knowing that You will hear and answer me in Jesus' name I pray, amen.

Additional Food Sources: 2 Kings 20:1-11, James 5:16, 1 Thessalonians 5:17-18

How is my prayer life?

_____

_____

_____

_____

_____

_____

_____

_____

_____

_____

_____

_____

What steps can I take to improve my prayer life?

_____

_____

_____

_____

_____

_____

_____

_____

_____

_____

Day 45

Food Source: Psalms 37:4 NIV

Food: *"Take delight in the Lord, and he will give you the desires of your heart."*

Nutrient: Delight for Desires

Digestion: Our food today has a condition. If you take delight in the Lord then He will give you the desires of your heart. Delight means to take great pleasure in. You have a role to play and God has His role to play. Your role comes first in this case, to delight in the Lord. After you have done that then He will give you the desires of your heart. If we delight in the Lord we will:

- Seek to get closer to Him daily by reading the Word, praying and fasting.
- We will aim to please Him by obeying His Word.
- We will serve Him with our praise and worship, our resources, our service to others and our service to build His kingdom.

If we delight in God then His desires will become our desires. He will have no problem giving us these desires because they are also His desires. For months I wrestled with the idea of selling my first car because I thought I couldn't afford a new one at the time, but one day God said to me, it is time to upgrade. Because I delight myself in Him He had the desire to give me a new car and placed that desire in my heart so it became my desire. Few months later I was able to purchase that car despite being told by the banks I would not be able to get the loan. Two days after I submitted my loan application, the loan was approved by the same bank that told me it was impossible.

God is Faithful to His Word and what is impossible with man is possible with Him! What godly desires do you have? Today let us exchange delight for desires. Delight in God and watch Him fulfill your desires.

Grocery Shopping: Father I thank You that You are a Faithful God who stands by Your Word. You promise that if I delight in You then You will give me the desires of my heart. Today, teach me how to delight in You and make it my desire. Make your desires my desires and as I delight in You, I pray that You will grant me the desires of my heart in Jesus' name I pray, amen.

Additional Food Sources: Job 22:26, Isaiah 58:14, Psalm 21:2, Psalm 145:19, Matthew 7:7-8

Have I been delighting in the Lord? Has He fulfilled any desire of my heart?

_____

_____

_____

_____

_____

_____

_____

_____

_____

_____

_____

What steps can I take to increase my delight in God?

_____

_____

_____

_____

_____

_____

_____

_____

_____

_____

Day 46

Food Source: James 1:2-4 NIV

Food: *"Consider it pure joy, my brothers and sisters, whenever you face trials of many kinds, because you know that the testing of your faith produces perseverance. Let perseverance finish its work so that you may be mature and complete, not lacking anything."*

Nutrient: Rejoice Through Trials

Digestion: We all face trials on a daily basis. Many of us complain when we do because the reality is nobody wants to go through any trial. But today the Lord is saying in our food, we should rejoice when we face trials of many kinds which is quite contrary. When we face different trials they test our faith and when our faith is tested it causes us to develop perseverance which is persistence in doing something despite delay or difficulty in achieving success.

When perseverance has completed its work we will be mature and complete not lacking anything. This is the place we want to get to! But it is a process. Just like you cannot get ice unless water is allowed to be properly frozen likewise we will not become mature unless we face trials, allow them to develop our perseverance and allow perseverance to complete its work.

135

Trials are so difficult for us to endure because of our attitude through it sometimes. Most of us get depressed which usually increase the difficulty because it usually invites its friend, sickness on board which is another story. Let us change our attitude today. God promises not to give us more that we can bare, to make the way of escape and never to leave us nor forsake us. So let us rejoice through our trials knowing also that all things work together for good to them that love God.

Grocery Shopping: Father, thank You for Your Word but this is not the easiest thing to do because we have our human nature to contend with. Give us Your peace today and your power to rejoice through whatever trials we are facing so that we can endure it and become mature and complete in Jesus' name I pray, amen.

Additional Food Sources: Romans 5:3-5, 1 Corinthians 10:13, Genesis 28:15, Romans 8:28

What is normally my attitude when I face trials?

_____
_____
_____
_____
_____
_____
_____
_____
_____
_____

What will I do to change my attitude when I face future trials?

_____
_____
_____
_____
_____
_____
_____
_____
_____
_____
_____

Day 47

Food Source: Proverbs 3:5-6 NKJV

Food: *"Trust in the LORD with all your heart, and lean not on your own understanding; In all your ways acknowledge Him, And He shall direct your paths."*

Nutrient: **Let God Direct Your Path**

Digestion: In 2015 when I discovered my mistake in marrying the wrong woman. I went to God in fasting and prayer for directions because I did not know what to do. For weeks I was seeing the number 55 and I was not sure why. One Sunday before going to church the Holy Spirit said to me, "Turn on the television." When I turned it on I saw Bishop Courtney McLean preaching. I watched until the end of the program and there the number was again, the address of his church WAFIF, 55 Old Harbour Road.

I felt a strong urge to visit the church because I needed to know why I was being lead to this church. The prophet, Samuel Fosu was scheduled to be there Wednesday to Friday of that week so based on my schedule I decided to visit on the Thursday. I did not know where that address was so I used google maps to find it. It turned out to be just up the road from where I was living and a church I had passed several times without noticing.

I have been going to WAFIF since then and the Lord has revealed all that was happening in my life, what I needed to do and my destiny. Because I trusted in God with all my heart and acknowledged Him in all my ways, today you are reading this book, I am divorced and remarried to my soulmate, I am a happy man and fulfilling my purpose. Today God wants you to do the same. Stop leaning to your own understanding, trust God with all your heart, acknowledge Him in everything and let Him direct your path.

Grocery Shopping: Father You are the best navigation system in existence. You will always get us to the right address at the right time. Help me to learn to trust You with all my heart today. Help me to stop leaning to my own understanding but to acknowledge You in all my ways so that You can direct my path in Jesus' name I pray, amen.

Additional Food Sources: Psalm 37:3-5, Proverbs 23:4, 1 Chronicles 28:9, Philippians 4:6

List times when God directed you and others
when you did your own thing.

_____

_____

_____

_____

_____

_____

_____

_____

_____

_____

Compare and analyze the results of God's
direction and your direction.

_____

_____

_____

_____

_____

_____

_____

_____

_____

_____

_____

Food Source: Hebrews 11:6 NKJV

Food: *"But without faith it is impossible to please Him, for he who comes to God must believe that He is, and that He is a rewarder of those who diligently seek Him."*

Nutrient: Exercise Your Faith

Digestion: A few years ago I faced some financial challenges. My car insurance expired and I did not have the money and did not want to ask anyone, maybe because of pride. However I decided that I was going to exercise my faith instead of parking my car and take the public transport. For two months I drove without insurance, praying every time before I moved for God's protection from accidents and for Him to provide the money to insure the car.

The money to insure the car did not come forth until two months later but I stayed in faith knowing that if He did not give me the money He would protect me and be my insurance until such time. Finally I was able to insure the car. I gave God thanks for protecting me and providing for me. About a day after I insured the car a policeman pulled me over to check my vehicle documents. I pulled over and gave them to Him with a big smile on my face. I said in my mind,

Lord You never cease to amaze me. My faith grew that day.

We cannot please God if we do not have faith and if you go to Him then you must believe that He rewards those that diligently seek Him. I am not encouraging anyone to do this because I had to repent since I found out it was illegal but not many people would because it takes faith. When a body builder wants to build his muscles he exercises them. Today if you want to increase your faith then you must exercise it, not necessarily the way I did but by stepping out in faith and pursuing something only God can reward you with in the natural and also by reading the Word of God. Exercise your faith!

Grocery Shopping: Father I thank you for reminding me that it is impossible to please You without faith. Thank You for giving me a measure of faith. Help me to exercise my faith so that it will be able to increase. You said that faith comes by hearing Your Word so help me to have a passion for Your Word and spend more time in it in Jesus' name I pray, amen.

Additional Food Sources: Hebrews 11:1-6, Romans 10:17, 12:3, 2 Peter 1:5-8

On a scale of 1 to 10, what level is my faith? Why is at this level?

_____
_____
_____
_____
_____
_____
_____
_____
_____
_____
_____

What steps can I take to exercise my faith so that it can grow?

_____
_____
_____
_____
_____
_____
_____
_____
_____
_____
_____
_____

Day 49

Food Source: Matthew 5:7 NKJV

Food: *"Blessed are the merciful, for they shall obtain mercy."*

Nutrient: Show Mercy

Digestion: Mercy is showing forgiveness to someone whom it is within your power to punish or harm. In Matthew 18 the parable is told of the unforgiving servant. He owed his master 10,000 bags of gold and was not able to pay. His master ordered that he, his wife and children be sold to repay this debt. He fell down on his face and begged the master to have patience until he could pay and the master had mercy on him and cancelled the debt.

The same servant that just received such great mercy, after he left, went out and found a fellow servant that owed him 100 silver coins, nothing compared to what he owed the master which was cancelled. He grabbed him and began to choke him saying pay me what you owe me. The servant begged just like he did but he showed him no mercy. He had him thrown into prison until he could pay.

When his master heard this he was angry and said to him, "You wicked servant! Should you not have shown this man the same mercy I showed you?" He was therefore handed over to be tortured until he could pay as well. Many of us are like this servant. We want mercy but refuse to show mercy but our food is saying only if we are merciful we will obtain mercy. Let us not be like this servant but let us show mercy to others.

Grocery Shopping: Father, I thank You that You are the epitome of mercy. Help me to be more like You, showing mercy to one another because Your Word says that I will only obtain mercy if I am merciful. In Jesus' name I pray, amen.

Additional Food Sources: Matthew 18:21-35

Can you recall times when God or others showed you mercy?

_____
_____
_____
_____
_____
_____
_____
_____
_____
_____
_____

Can you recall times when you did not show mercy when you should have? What will you do next time you are in a similar situation?

_____
_____
_____
_____
_____
_____
_____
_____
_____
_____

Day 50

Food Source: Philippians 4:13 NKJV

Food: *"I can do all things through Christ who strengthens me."*

Nutrient: You Can Do It

Digestion: In June 2016 the Lord gave me this task of doing a daily devotional and this format I use while doing a bible study. A month later He confirmed that this was what He wanted me to do through my spiritual father Bishop Courtney McLean. During a meeting with him, he said I think you should do a devotional. I told him I had actually started but I was not consistent as yet.

I was a bit concerned and in my mental capacity I could not see how I was going to consistently find a Word for every day. I knew that it would require serious dedication and commitment. I would also be setting myself up because I have already created an atmosphere for the devotional and the expectation was very high. Whenever I was late or didn't send a devotional I would receive a message from someone asking, what happened?

In my own strength I just knew it wasn't possible but I prayed and said "God if this is what you need me to do; I know you will give me the strength to do it." Today marks my 50th ANNIVERSARY! Yes I have done 50 Devotionals!

147

It has become easier because of His strength! Today I want to let you know that whatever it is that God has called you to do: Serve in His kingdom, start a business, further your education, whatever it is, you can do it too because He will give you the strength to! Put away fear and take that step of faith today, you can do it!

Grocery Shopping: Father I am thankful that all things are possible with you. In my own strength this task (say the task) seems impossible but today I am going to trust Your strength because I know I can do all things through You who strengthen me. I rebuke the spirit of fear and I command my faith to arise in Jesus' name I pray, amen.

Additional Food Sources: Psalm 28:7, 2 Corinthians 12:9-10, Isaiah 40:29-31

What task(s) has God given me to do and what is preventing me from doing it?

_____
_____
_____
_____
_____
_____
_____
_____
_____
_____

What steps will I take to start doing this/these task(s)?

_____
_____
_____
_____
_____
_____
_____
_____
_____
_____
_____

Day 51

Food Source: Psalms 127:3 NKJV

Food: *"Behold, children are a heritage from the LORD, The fruit of the womb is a reward."*

Nutrient: **Appreciate Your Heritage and Reward**

Digestion: My son celebrated his 6th birthday September 17, 2016 and I was just thankful to God for my inheritance, my reward and the joy of fatherhood. The day of his birth was one of the happiest days of my life. Unfortunately I was not able to be there to watch him come into this world because he was born in St. Kitts but 2 weeks later I held him for the first time. I remember staring at him with a big smile on my face and thanking God that he was perfectly created. My life had changed, I was now a father.

I understood the relationship that God has with His son Jesus. It helped me to appreciate the crucifixion and the love God has for me because if I had to sacrifice my son it would be a big oh no! I love him too much; I don't even want a mosquito to bite him. But God had to bear that agony to watch His only begotten son crucified to save you and me. I can imagine how heart broken and hurt He felt when Jesus cried "My God, my God, why have you forsaken me?"

Solomon says in our food that children are a heritage. God gives them to us. Many people are trying to have children and cannot, others have and don't appreciate them instead they abuse and hurt them. Some people get pregnant and say it is a mistake and go as far as abortion but God does not make mistakes. A child is a blessing. Appreciate your heritage from your Father today.

Grocery Shopping: Father I thank You for the joy of parenthood. Thank You for blessing me with the fruit of the womb. Those who have not yet received, I pray that You will grant it unto them. I appreciate my heritage and ask that you help me to be a better parent today. Cover my children under Your blood, put Your mark on them and bless them in every aspect of life! I declare that they are blessed and will be mighty on this earth in Jesus' name I pray, amen.

Additional Food Sources: Psalm 127:3-5, Psalm 112:2, Proverbs 17:6

What lessons did I learn from this message?

_____
_____
_____
_____
_____
_____
_____
_____
_____
_____

What are my action plans?

_____
_____
_____
_____
_____
_____
_____
_____
_____
_____
_____
_____

Day 52

Food Source: Genesis 4:4 NKJV

Food: *"Abel also brought of the firstborn of his flock and of their fat. And the LORD respected Abel and his offering,"*

Nutrient: Give First Fruit, Cheerfully

Digestion: In Genesis 4 the story is told of Cain and Abel, each giving an offering to God. Abel was a shepherd and Cain was a tiller of the ground. So Cain brought an offering of the fruit of the ground. Abel brought an offering of the firstborn of his flock and of their fat. God respected Abel and his offering but He did not respect Cain or his offering.

Abel and his offering were respected because of two things: his attitude in giving and the type of offering he gave. He was a cheerful giver and he gave God his best. God loves a cheerful giver. His offering was a first fruit offering. A first fruit is the first produce of the harvest. Cain's harvest in this case was that of fruits but Abel's harvest was of sheep therefore his first fruit was the firstborn of his flock.

God is good to us. He provides so many opportunities for us and blesses us in so many ways. We should practice honoring Him with our first fruit. That is, giving him the first of what we earn or receive and do it with a cheerful heart. He

153

only asks for 10%. When we do this God will respect our offering and He promises to give back to us in abundance. Give Him your first fruit and do it cheerfully.

Grocery Shopping: Father I thank You that all good gifts around us are sent from heaven above. You deserve our first fruit and our willing and cheerful giving for Your goodness towards us. Help us today to start honoring You with our first fruit and with the right attitude in Jesus' name I pray, amen.

Additional Food Sources: Genesis 4:3-5, 2 Corinthians 9:7, Proverbs 3:9-10, Exodus 22:29, Malachi 3:10

Have I been honoring God with my first fruit? Why?

_____
_____
_____
_____
_____
_____
_____
_____
_____
_____

What is my action plan to always honor God with my first fruit?

_____
_____
_____
_____
_____
_____
_____
_____
_____
_____
_____

Day 53

Food Source: James 4:3 NIV

Food: *"When you ask, you do not receive, because you ask with wrong motives, that you may spend what you get on your pleasures."*

Nutrient: Ask With the Right Motives

Digestion: Jesus said, "For everyone who asks receives..." Sometimes however, we ask God for some things and we do not receive them and we may ask the question; why do we ask and not receive when Jesus said everyone who asks receives? Our food today highlights one of the reasons we do not receive when we ask. James says that: When you ask, you do not receive, because you ask with wrong motives, that you may spend what you get on your pleasures.

So the answer to that question is; you are asking with the wrong motives! I heard the testimony of a brother who said his father used to take his salary to the bar and spend it off on alcohol. The family could only get money from him if they caught him before he went to the bar or whatever they could find after he was drunk and they searched his pocket. This is a classic example of wrong motive and spending what you get on your pleasures.

God will not give us the things we ask for when we have such motives. The right motive is (1) Unselfish and (2) Causes God to be glorified. When God blesses us He wants us to bless others. We must thank Him and testify of His goodness towards us, we must glorify Him. Before we ask today let us evaluate the motive, if it is not right then don't waste your time because you will not receive. Ask with the right motive!

Grocery Shopping: Father I thank You for highlighting today, one of the reasons we do receive when we ask. Help me to make the necessary adjustment today and apply this Word to my life. Help me to ask with the right motive, to bless others and to glorify you in Jesus' name I pray, amen.

Additional Food Sources: Matthew 7:8, Job 27:8-9, Psalm 66:18, Proverbs 15:29

Have I been asking with the right motives?

_____

_____

_____

_____

_____

_____

_____

_____

_____

_____

How can I ensure that I always have the right motives?

_____

_____

_____

_____

_____

_____

_____

_____

_____

_____

_____

_____

Day 54

Food Source: II Corinthians 5:17 NKJV

Food: *"Therefore, if anyone is in Christ, he is a new creation; old things have passed away; behold, all things have become new."*

Nutrient: God Wants to Make You New

Digestion: Few years ago I was heading in the wrong direction. I found myself living promiscuously, partying, drinking and doing the things that I knew were not right. I grew up in church and had a passion for the Word of God because apparently He had His mark on me. I used to annoy my best friend because I would quote a scripture to him for everything, sometimes to justify my sinful behavior.

But in 2013 God finally convicted me and I had to surrender my life to Him because I examined my life and I knew that was not His will for my life. I became a new person. I hated the things that I used to love doing. I tried drinking a beer and my body totally rejected it. I became a loyal husband. In fact infidelity is probably one of the things I hate the most. I now believe we should be faithful to God and our spouse regardless of the situation.

When you come in contact with Jesus your life can never be the same! Old things are passed away and behold all things become new. It does not happen overnight and our sinful nature does not make it any easier. It is a process but if you obey God, live by his Word and continually confess your sins to Him and repent, eventually He will cleanse you from your sinful nature. His Grace is sufficient to make you new no matter where that bad path led you. Will you allow Him to make you new today? God Wants to Make You New!

Grocery Shopping: Father I thank You for Your Grace, Your love for me and Your desire to save me and make me new. I recognize that life is meaningless without You! I give up all my old ways today, make me new and a reflection of You in Jesus' name I pray, amen.

Additional Food Sources: Isaiah 43:18-19, Romans 8:9-11, 10:8-9, 1 John 1:8-9, John 3:16, 1 Corinthians 10:13

What are the things that I need to change in my life?

_____

_____

_____

_____

_____

_____

_____

_____

_____

_____

What steps can I take to make the transformation necessary?

_____

_____

_____

_____

_____

_____

_____

_____

_____

_____

Food Source: 1 Corinthians 11:3 NIV

Food: *"But I want you to realize that the head of every man is Christ, and the head of the woman is man, and the head of Christ is God."*

Nutrient: Respect God's Hierarchy

Digestion: After surrendering to Christ, one of the most important things to learn and adhere to is God's hierarchy, His order of authority. Many struggle with this issue because they have not fully surrendered to Him. When we are fully surrendered to Christ we must become sheep. The important character to emulate is that a sheep only follows the shepherd and do as instructed.

Our food outlines God's hierarchy which was instituted from creation. Because of disobedience and sin by Adam and Eve this hierarchy was disturbed. One of the punishments outlined for their sin was that the woman will try to control the man but the man will rule over her. Therefore Paul reiterates the hierarchy here. God is the head of Christ, Christ is the head of man and man is the head of woman.

Some men use this authority to lord over women but that was never God's intention as the relationship was meant to be a partnership that yields oneness. As a result God has also established rules to restrict such abusive tendencies. Peter says that the husband should respect his wife as the weaker vessel that his prayers may not be hindered. So Wives respect and submit to your husbands, husbands respect and love your wives. Can you breathe without oxygen? You cannot please God if you don't obey His Word. Let us respect God's hierarchy.

Grocery Shopping: Father, You are the same yesterday, today and forever more. Your hierarchy was established and will remain in effect whether we choose to obey or not. My desire is to please You so help me to be a sheep, help me to obey Your Word and respect Your hierarchy in Jesus' name I pray, amen.

Additional Food Sources: Genesis 3:16, John 10:27, 1 Peter 3:7, Ephesians 5:22-33

List ways I have been disrespecting God's Hierarchy.

_____
_____
_____
_____
_____
_____
_____
_____
_____
_____

List corrective methods to take.

_____
_____
_____
_____
_____
_____
_____
_____
_____
_____
_____

Day 56

Food Source: Matthew 22:37-38 NIV

Food: *"Jesus replied: "Love the Lord your God with all your heart and with all your soul and with all your mind.' This is the first and greatest commandment."*

Nutrient: The First and Greatest Commandment

Digestion: Because the Pharisees heard that Jesus had silenced the Sadducees, they came together to test Jesus. One of them, who was an expert in the law, asked Him the question, "Teacher, which is the greatest commandment in the law?" Jesus responded by saying 'Love the Lord your God with all your heart and with all your soul and with all your mind.' He also told them that this is the first and greatest commandment.

So the first and greatest commandment is that we love God but not just love Him, we should do it with all our heart, soul and mind. The heart deals with our emotions, the soul deals with our spirituality and the mind deals with our thoughts. We should always express our love for God through our worship and service for Him and to others. Whatever we do for Him we must do it whole heartedly.

165

We should always keep our thoughts focused on Him by reading His Word daily and seeking to have a closer relationship with Him. When we do this we will please God because we will not sin against Him and we will love one another. Loving God this way means that you: Seek to know Him through His Word; try to please Him by obeying His Word and honoring Him in every aspect of your life. We can honor God by giving the required tithes and offerings, treating each other with love and living by His Word. Today let us love God but with all our heart, soul and mind because it is the first and greatest commandment.

Grocery Shopping: Father I thank You that You loved us first. Help us to love You today but not just with our lips but with our whole heart, our soul and our mind. This is the love that You commanded of us. Teach me how to love You this way in Jesus' name I pray, amen.

Additional Food Sources: Deuteronomy 6:5, 10:12-13, 30:6

How is my love radar towards God?

_____
_____
_____
_____
_____
_____
_____
_____
_____
_____
_____

What practical steps can I take to increase my love for God?

_____
_____
_____
_____
_____
_____
_____
_____
_____
_____
_____

Day 57

Food Source: Matthew 22:39-40 NLT

Food: *"A second is equally important: 'Love your neighbor as yourself.' The entire law and all the demands of the prophets are based on these two commandments."*

Nutrient: **Fulfill the Entire Law through Love**

Digestion: The second greatest commandment that Jesus told the Pharisees is to love your neighbor as yourself. He then told them that the entire law and all the demands of the prophets are based on these two commandments, love for God and love for one another. The bible says that love is the greatest and it covers a multitude of sins therefore this is no surprise.

There has been much confusion about the Old and New Testament and what laws are applicable to believers today. Testament is a covenant. So the old covenant was established between God and Israel to govern their relationship. This covenant was insufficient therefore Jesus was sent to die for us and a new covenant was established. Only the laws of the old covenant that are re-instated in the new covenant are applicable to believers under this new covenant.

Paul says that the entire law is fulfilled even in this one commandment; love your neighbor as yourself. If we love our neighbors as ourselves then the other laws would be achieved because we would not murder, commit adultery, steal, bear false witness or covet our neighbors. Today let us fulfill the entire law through love, love for God and love for one another.

Grocery Shopping: Father, help us to realize that love is the solution to most of the problems we face in our society today. Pour out Your agape love, that unconditional love upon us today. Help us to love You and love our neighbors as ourselves today in Jesus' name I pray, amen.

Additional Food Sources: 1 Corinthians 13:13, 1 Peter 4:8, Hebrews 10:4, Galatians 5:14, Romans 13:10

Have I been loving my neighbors? How have I been showing this love to them?

_____

_____

_____

_____

_____

_____

_____

_____

_____

_____

_____

What steps can I take to ensure that I always love my neighbors?

_____

_____

_____

_____

_____

_____

_____

_____

_____

_____

_____

_____

Day 58

Food Source: 1 Corinthians 10:13 NIV

Food: *"No temptation has overtaken you except what is common to mankind. And God is faithful; he will not let you be tempted beyond what you can bear. But when you are tempted, he will also provide a way out so that you can endure it."*

Nutrient: God Provides a Way Out of Temptation

Digestion: Some time ago I faced my greatest temptation. At the time I was living with my ex-wife, a woman that I did not wish to be around or even see at that time because we were separated. She did everything in her power to make me lose it and do something I would regret but thanks be to God I was able to resist the temptation. I had asked her not to take a particular person to my house but she did it anyway.

One day I came home early to pick up something. As I drove up I saw her with the person I asked her not to take to the house. I was furious but God made me only say good evening in response to the person, picked up what I came for and left. As I drove away I said, "God why don't you let this woman drop down and die and come out of my life?!" When I realized what I had said, I quickly repented because the Bible says to abstain from all appearance of evil. I said "Lord you know I don't mean that but I am bitter! Why do you allow this woman to continue to be in my space and tempting me to sin?! Please move her out of my way!"

The same night when I got back home I got a message from her that she needed to talk to me. The next day we had that talk and she told me that she was moving out of the house. About two days later she moved out. God's Word is tested and proven! He is still faithful today; He will not let you be tempted beyond what you can bear. But when you are tempted, He will also provide a way out so that you can endure it. Don't yield to temptation! Will you Trust His Word and be patient? God will provide a way out of your temptation.

Grocery Shopping: Father we acknowledge that temptation will always come because even Jesus was tempted while He was on earth but He overcame. He rebuked the devil and he fled. We have that same power today. Help us not to yield to temptation but help us to escape and overcome them in Jesus' name I pray, amen.

Additional Food Sources: 1 Thessalonians 5:22, James 4:7, Matthew 4:1-11

What temptations am I facing?

_____

_____

_____

_____

_____

_____

_____

_____

_____

_____

_____

What steps I can take to overcome these temptations?

_____

_____

_____

_____

_____

_____

_____

_____

_____

_____

_____

_____

Day 59

Food Source: Hebrews 8:12 NLT

Food: *"And I will forgive their wickedness, and I will never again remember their sins."*

Nutrient: God Forgets Repented Sins

Digestion: One of the reasons unsaved people have difficulty surrendering to Christ is the ignorance of His mercy. This is also the reason why some Christians backslide. God is a God of Judgment but he is also a God of mercy and forgiveness. Jesus is well aware of our sinful nature and the challenges we face because He came on earth to live in flesh so that He could experience what we experience.

He knows that the heart of man is desperately wicked and He knows that we all have sinned and come short of His glory. Sin is a reproach unto us. God turns his face away from us when sin is present in our lives. That is why we need to confess our sins and repent daily. When we do this, He promises as our food states to forgive us and forget our sins.

God does not hold past sins against us or torment us with the memories. That is the job of the devil to keep you in bondage and make you a slave to sin. Take control today! Remind the devil of Romans 8:1-2. There is no condemnation to those who are in Christ Jesus who walk not after the

174

flesh but after the spirit because he has made you free from sin.

Confess your sins, repent of them, forgive yourself and be at peace knowing that God has forgiven you and He forgets repented sins.

Grocery Shopping: Father I thank You that You search the heart and test the mind and You give every man according to his ways and the fruit of his deeds. When I confess my sins to You, You promise to cleanse me from all unrighteousness and forget my sins. Help me to understand and accept this Grace and mercy. I confess my sins (say them) to You today in Jesus' name I pray, amen.

Additional Food Sources: Jeremiah 17:9-10, Romans 3:23, Proverbs 14:34, Isaiah 59:2, 1 John 1:9, Romans 8:1-2

Ask God to search your heart and show you the things in your life that displeases Him and record them.

_____
_____
_____
_____
_____
_____
_____
_____
_____
_____
_____

List steps to repent of the things that displease Him.

_____
_____
_____
_____
_____
_____
_____
_____
_____
_____

Day 60

Food Source: Hebrews 11:1 NKJV

Food: *"Now faith is the substance of things hoped for, the evidence of things not seen."*

Nutrient: God Fulfills His Promises Part 1: When We Exercise Faith

Digestion: In 2016 I thought about selling my car to pay off some of my debts and buy a cheaper one but I wrestled with the idea of going backwards so I dismissed the idea. Few months later, while going home one night in total silence, the Holy Spirit spoke to me and told me that it was time to sell the car and upgrade. When I got home I did the math and it looked possible so I got fired up and started to move towards it.

I sense that God was telling me to go back to the lady at the bank that processed my last loan. I searched for her number but I could not remember her name so I went to bed. The next morning I woke up thinking about my plan and as I was there washing, the Holy Spirit told me her name. I looked in my contacts for the name and there it was. After the weekend, I called her and then went to the car dealer to look at the car I was interested in and got a quote. When I went to the bank to meet with her and she did the necessary calculations she told me that it was not possible to get a loan to purchase the new car until I sold my car and paid off another loan that I had.

I left the bank feeling disappointed but not defeated because I am a man of faith. This is where a lot of us give up at the first sign of failure and the devil is happy. You have to understand that failure is temporary defeat! God wants us to have faith because it is the substance, the physical existence of the things we hope for and the evidence that it is ours even though we can't see it yet. We must exercise faith if we want God to fulfill His promises to us. Will you exercise your faith today? Do the natural; God will do the supernatural for you!

Grocery Shopping: Father without faith it is impossible to please You. There are so many different situations in the bible where your hand was moved to take action all because of the faith of these people. Help me to understand that all You want me to do is to have faith in You and do what I need to do and You will do the things that I cannot do. Help me to lift my faith and exercise it in Jesus' name I pray, amen.

Additional Food Sources: Hebrews 11:4-7

What lessons did I learn from this message?

_____
_____
_____
_____
_____
_____
_____
_____
_____
_____
_____

List the things that cause your faith to diminish.

_____
_____
_____
_____
_____
_____
_____
_____
_____
_____
_____
_____

Day 61

Food Source: Deuteronomy 18:22 NIV

Food: *"If what a prophet proclaims in the name of the Lord does not take place or come true, that is a message the Lord has not spoken. That prophet has spoken presumptuously, so do not be alarmed."*

Nutrient: **God Fulfills His Promises Part 2: He Will Confirm His Word**

Digestion: After leaving the bank I started to brain storm other ways to get that new car. I started to check the car dealers for used cars and eventually I found one that was being shipped and would take a few weeks to get to Jamaica. I made the necessary enquiries and decided to work with that one because I liked it and it would give me some time to get my car sold.

About two weeks later, I went to church at WAFIF. The prophet Frank Udoh was there that Sunday and he prophesied to me. As he was walking by, he stopped and said, "I smell favor on you. I see you registering a new car." He laid his hands on my head and said, "The Grace has been released for you to get that car." God had confirmed His Word to me and I knew that He would fulfill His promise.

When God speaks to us He will also give us confirmation, sometimes in the form of a prophecy. What our food is basically saying today is that if you get a prophecy and you are not sure if it was a message from God you can easily prove it. If what was prophesied actually comes true it was a message from God. If it does not then it was not a message from God. Few months later I registered that new car. Is God instructing you to do something? Move by faith! Are you in doubt? Ask for confirmation because God will confirm His Word and fulfill His promise.

Grocery Shopping: Father I thank you that You are a God who confirms Your Word because if You said it, it must be done! I rebuke every source of confusion and lack of faith. I declare clarification and confirmation. Let faith arise and cause your people to be encouraged to press towards that which you have prophesied concerning their future by prophecy or promises made in Your Word in Jesus name, amen!

Additional Food Sources: Jeremiah 28:9, Romans 3:4, Numbers 23:19

What promise am I believing God to fulfill in my life?

_____
_____
_____
_____
_____
_____
_____
_____
_____
_____

What are the steps to be taken to make this a reality?

_____
_____
_____
_____
_____
_____
_____
_____
_____
_____
_____

Day 62

Food Source: 1 Timothy 1:18 NIV

Food: *"Timothy, my son, I am giving you this command in keeping with the prophecies once made about you, so that by recalling them you may fight the battle well,"*

Nutrient: God Fulfills His Promises Part 3: Fight for Your Blessings

Digestion: After receiving my prophecy about the car I had to fight for it. You see, the devil's job is always to rob us of our blessings so you need to fight because if you don't, the devil will steal your blessings. Paul was saying to Timothy in our food; keep in mind what was prophesied about you because when you do this you will fight the battle well. Few weeks later, the car that I was interested in came. So I went to look at it and to make a deposit. I spoke with loan officer from another bank at the car mart and after analyzing my financial situation she basically told me that it was impossible to get a loan of that magnitude to purchase the car I wanted even if I sold my car and paid off the loan I had. She advised me to choose a cheaper car but I was determined that it was the car I wanted but I listened to her suggestion. I left the car mart and went back to my office. Still not feeling defeated because I recalled my prophecy.

I went back on the dealer's website and found a better car with all the features that I wanted and even more. When I called the dealer for the price it was J$200,000 less than the other car but it was still in Japan and would not arrive until a month time. So I called back the loan officer that God had revealed the name to me and she told me that it was possible but I would have to sell the car first and pay off the loan. So the next day I went back to the car dealer and made my deposit on that car! I had gotten two offers for my car but they were too low so I refused them. The car came and it was not sold but recalling my prophecy I continued in faith and fight. I got all the documentation and sent through the loan application despite what the loan officer told me because that was what the Lord told me to do. The application was submitted on a Thursday and by the Monday she called me to inform me that my loan has been approved! When I called the sales rep. he told me that he heard the loan was approved but a man was waiting for me to "drop the catch" to buy my car. The devil is a liar! Is anything impossible for God? Take the limits off God!! He is not limited by your resources or who you know. Fight for your blessings and the fulfilment of your prophecies!

Grocery Shopping: Father I give you all the glory today for my testimony, nothing is impossible for You! I pray that it will encourage

184

someone today to fight for what was prophesied to them or for the promises that are written in Your Word in Jesus' name I pray, amen.

Additional Food Sources: John 10:10, Matthew 19:26

What are the limits that I have placed on God in light of my current situations?

_____
_____
_____
_____
_____
_____
_____
_____
_____

What are the steps I can take to remove these limitations?

_____
_____
_____
_____
_____
_____
_____
_____
_____

Day 63

Food Source: Matthew 7:7-8 NKJV

Food: *"Ask, and it will be given to you; seek, and you will find; knock, and it will be opened to you. For everyone who asks receives, and he who seeks finds, and to him who knocks it will be opened."*

Nutrient: **God Fulfills His Promises Part 4: Ask, Seek and Knock**

Digestion: The loan was approved but the car was not yet sold and I needed the money from the sale to complete the transaction. One of my prayers however, was that God allowed me to complete the process without the inconvenience of not having a car to drive, one of the reasons I did not accept the offers that I got. The loan officer was pushing me to move and others were telling me that they would have to sell the car first, if they were in my position. I decided to stay in faith and ride the wave because God was working it for my good. My only option was to seek help so I decided to ask for help.

Our food says we should ask because everyone who asks receives, we should seek because everyone who seeks find, and we should knock because the door will be opened to us. I wish I could help someone to see the power of these verses. The verses say "will" not maybe! A lot of

186

people are depressed and alone in their storm because of fear and pride which hinders them from accessing the power of these verses through asking, seeking and knocking. They are afraid to hear no! You will only hear no if you ask, seek or knock on the wrong door or at the wrong time. It means that you need to find the right one because Jesus said you will receive, you will find and the door will be opened.

The first person I asked was unable to help but my other friend said yes so I was able to drive my new car home few days later. God fulfills His promise! You see God has placed destiny helpers in our lives to help us to get to where He wants to take us. No means you need to find the right person, your destiny helper, because He promised that you will. The sooner you realize this, the sooner you will put away that fear and pride and start to ask, seek and knock because you WILL receive, you WILL find and the door WILL be opened. Will you try it today?

Grocery Shopping: Father my soul cries out Hallelujah today! Thank You for fulfilling Your promise to me. I pray that my testimony will open the eyes of those reading today and cause faith to arise! I rebuke the spirit of fear and pride in the name of Jesus because You have not given us a spirit of fear and You detest the proud. Give us the boldness to ask, seek and knock so that we will receive, we will find and the door will be opened in Jesus' name I pray, amen.

Additional Food Sources: James 4:2-6, John 14:13-14, 2 Timothy 1:7

What are the things that I have stopped asking for because of disappointments?

_____
_____
_____
_____
_____
_____
_____
_____

List the things that you are believing God for.

_____
_____
_____
_____
_____
_____
_____
_____
_____
_____

Day 64

Food Source: I Corinthians 2:9 NKJV

Food: *"But as it is written: "Eye has not seen, nor ear heard, nor have entered into the heart of man the things which God has prepared for those who love Him."*

Nutrient: **God Fulfills His Promises Part 5: Love God and Be Surprised!**

Digestion: Finally I drove my new car out of the car mart and my heart was just filled with thanksgiving and love for God for His faithfulness towards me! I don't know what I have done to deserve it but one thing I can do is testify so that He will be glorified! I feel so blessed but our food this morning is telling me that I have not seen anything yet! God has great surprises for those who love Him.

Few months ago I wrestled with the idea of being downgraded because one of my mantra is forward ever and backward never. I thought I had to sell my car in order to pay off my debts but one day I got still and He was able to speak to me and He said the opposite, upgrade! When He said upgrade I thought I had to sell my car in order to upgrade but the loan was approved without me having to do that. I now had two cars and based on what God was saying to me, my mind set had changed.

I am putting no more limits on my God! He has made His point clear to me! If I delight myself in Him He will give me the desires of my heart! His plans for me are bigger and greater than my imagination. I had only been a Christian for 3 years and 6 months at the time, still a toddler! But I tell you, it is not as hard as I had thought, indeed His yoke is easy and His burden is light. His anger is for a moment but His favor is for life.

Do you love God? If your answer is yes then you are in for a Surprise! If the answer is anything other than yes then today you need to do something about that, love God and be surprised!

Grocery Shopping: Father, great is thy faithfulness unto me! All I have needed your hands have provided! I give You glory and honor with my testimony today. Let it ignite the faith of Your people. Let someone experience a new love for You today! Show them a sign of what You have in store for those who love You, in Jesus' name I pray, amen.

Additional Food Sources: Matthew 11:30, Psalm 30:5

What are the things that I am putting a limit on God for?

_____
_____
_____
_____
_____
_____
_____
_____
_____
_____
_____

What is my action plan to take the limits off God?

_____
_____
_____
_____
_____
_____
_____
_____
_____
_____
_____
_____
_____

Day 65

Food Source: II Peter 1:3 NKJV

Food: *"as His divine power has given to us all things that pertain to life and godliness, through the knowledge of Him who called us by glory and virtue,"*

Nutrient: Convert Your Potential to Product (Po to Pro)

Digestion: All of us have potential which is the capacity to become or develop something. This potential has been given to us by God to convert into a product which is a person or thing that is the result of an action or process. Peter said in our food that God has given to us all the things that pertain to life and godliness. This means that the gifts, skills or talents and the resources that you need to convert your potential to product have been released to you from birth. Your potential now requires a **DAD**, **D**iscovery, **A**ctivation and **D**etermination to become a product.

Discovery - Few years ago I discovered that I had the gift of writing after I was forced to write a strong letter to a particular school regarding a situation with my ex-wife. The letter produced a solution the same day it was received. This came as a surprise because most of my school life, English was never my favorite subject. Gifts can

192

be discovered in many ways but they are in you so start paying more attention. What are you good at? What are you passionate about?

Activation- After discovering your gifts you need to activate them. This may mean that you need to enroll into a course of study to develop them. After discovering that I was a writer and that God wanted me to write messages I decided to enroll into Preaching 101 at the Courtney McLean School of Ministry. By the time I completed the 1st module; the Lord told me to write this daily devotion and gave me this format. You are now reading the 1st of 4 volumes of my book **Spiritual Food**. I also graduated from Preaching 101 as valedictorian. What step do you need to take to activate and develop your gift?

Determination- You may get discouraged at the first sign of failure. You may even have fear that prevents you from making the first step. My challenge was how I will get a Word every day to do a daily devotion. God will give you the Grace to do anything that He has called you to do so you just need to trust His strength and persevere until you convert your Po to Pro. Po to Pro is a lifetime process! When you have become or created a product, the potential is always in you to create or become a greater product. Your ability to become wealthy and you fulfilling your purpose depends on this process so start it today.

Grocery Shopping: Father we thank You for giving us the potential to become products. Help those of us who have not yet discovered, to discover our potential. Give us the Grace to activate them and the determination to go from Po to Pro. As we go through this process grant us products that will improve the lives of others and as a result are high in demand. Cause these products to enhance your kingdom, make us wealthy and add no sorrow to our lives in Jesus' name I pray, amen.

Additional Food Sources: Proverbs 10:4, 12:24, 13:4, 19:15, 21:5

What potentials do I have?

_____
_____
_____
_____
_____
_____
_____
_____
_____
_____
_____

What steps do I need to take to convert them to products?

_____
_____
_____
_____
_____
_____
_____
_____
_____
_____
_____
_____
_____

Day 66

Food Source: Numbers 16:20-21 NKJV

Food: *"And the LORD spoke to Moses and Aaron, saying, "Separate yourselves from among this congregation, that I may consume them in a moment."*

Nutrient: God Will Consume the Wicked in a Moment

Digestion: Korah had formed a company and rebelled against Moses and Aaron their leader. In doing so, they also rebelled against God and made Him angry. In our food He said to Moses and Aaron, "Separate yourselves from among this congregation, that I may consume them in a moment." They had to fall down on their faces and ask God not to allow the sin of one man to cause Him to destroy the whole congregation.

God loves us but if we continue to rebel against God and His Word, He is going to separate the righteous and execute judgment upon the wicked!

God usually gives us a warning and chance of repentance before His judgement. Several warnings have gone forth and the wicked have not repented. God is being merciful because of the cry of the righteous to Him. Israel and Korah's company was spared that moment because of the cry of Moses and Aaron. God later instructed Moses however, to tell the congregation to separate from these wicked men: Korah, Dathan and Abiram because they did not repent.

He then opened the earth and it swallowed these three alive with all their households and their goods. He then consumed the other 250 men who were offering incense with fire.

The cry of the righteous will not always spare the wicked! Every man has to give an account for his own sins and repent. We may have been spared from many disasters but a day will come when God is going to separate the righteous and consume the wicked in a moment.

Grocery Shopping: Father, You are a God of love but also a God of judgment. You usually give us a warning and chance of repentance before You send Your righteous judgement. Several warnings have gone forth but I pray that You will not harden the hearts of Your people like Pharaoh but allow them to take heed to Your Word and repent of their wicked ways to avert Your judgment in Jesus' name I pray, amen.

Additional Food Sources: Numbers 16:1-40, Isaiah 26:21, Psalm 37:38, Romans 2:1-11

What are the things that I need to separate myself from?

_____
_____
_____
_____
_____
_____
_____
_____
_____
_____
_____

What are my action plans?

_____
_____
_____
_____
_____
_____
_____
_____
_____
_____
_____
_____
_____
_____

Day 67

Food Source: Matthew 6:33 KJV

Food: *"But seek ye first the kingdom of God, and his righteousness; and all these things shall be added unto you."*

Nutrient: Seek and Find Him Today

Digestion: I do believe in prosperity and that we should enjoy life while we are on earth. If our Father is a King then it means that we are princes and princesses and we should live as such. I have been to quite a few funerals however and you are only allowed one suit. Someone else will enjoy all the material things that you dedicate your time trying to acquire in this life. The body that we try so hard to keep in shape and maintain will be a sumptuous meal for some worms one day.

Hell is real my friend! Dives, the rich man in Luke 16, experienced it and when he realized how terrible it was he begged Abraham to warn his other brothers not to come to this place! But Abraham told him that if they can't believe Moses and the prophets they won't believe one that rises from the dead. I don't know about you but I refuse to be a Thomas. I don't have to see hell with mine own eyes to know that it is real. The heat I feel from the sun and the excruciating pain from hot oil burns when cooking and from the steam of the iron when pressing is enough to convince me that I don't need to be at that place.

Only your soul is important, that is why the bible asks the question, what does it profit a man to gain this whole world and lose his own soul? The end is near my friend, the things that you see happening are the fulfillment of end time prophecies. If Jesus is not your pilot you need to seek Him while He can be found. The material things you crave will be given to you and you are also promised eternal life but the condition is that you must Seek God and His righteousness first. If Jesus is your pilot don't be selfish, help someone else to find Him. Today I want you to ask yourself this question: Are the things preventing me from being a child of God worth me losing my soul? I can answer that for you. No they are not! Seek and Find Him today.

Grocery Shopping: Father I thank You for sending Your son Jesus to suffer and die to save me. I will not let His suffering be in vain. I want You to be my pilot today. I want You to take me to my destination and I want it to be heaven, not hell. Forgive me of my sins and make my heart Your home today. I surrender my life to You in Jesus' name I pray, amen.

Additional Food Sources: Ecclesiastes 2:18-26, 12:13-14, Luke 16:19-31, Matthew 16:26, John 3:16

What are the things preventing me from surrendering my life to Jesus Christ? Are they worth me losing my soul?

_____
_____
_____
_____
_____
_____
_____
_____
_____
_____
_____
_____

What steps can I take to surrender totally to Jesus today?

_____
_____
_____
_____
_____
_____
_____
_____
_____
_____
_____
_____
_____
_____

Day 68

Food Source: Exodus 20:17 KJV

Food: *"Thou shalt not covet thy neighbor's house, thou shalt not covet thy neighbor's wife, nor his manservant, nor his maidservant, nor his ox, nor his ass, nor any thing that is thy neighbor's."*

Nutrient: **Celebrate Your Neighbours, You Are Next**

Digestion: Some months ago my neighbor and friend sold his car to purchase a new car. He was out of a car for a few weeks. I had to assist him with transportation during this period. Some days I had to leave for work earlier than desired but it was not a problem. One day while going to work we found a nice car in a car mart and I encouraged him to get it. Shortly thereafter he was able to finalize the deal.

I was in the process of getting a new car as well but it was taking longer than I expected but God's timing is always right. One morning while washing my car I began to look around and count the neighbours that had bought new vehicles since we moved into the community. It was five. I began to thank God that he is in the neighborhood and that I am next in line for my blessing. I declared that I will be number six. A few weeks later I was able to purchase my new car too.

This is a principle that we should learn to embrace, to celebrate our neighbours' blessings. The fact that God is in the neighborhood, it simply means that you may be next in line for your blessing. Our food is saying that we should not covet our neighbours' possessions because we really don't need to. This can prevent us from receiving our blessings. We should love our neighbours as we love ourselves and desire the best for them. The right attitude to have is to celebrate your neighbours' success because you may be next in line for your blessings.

Grocery Shopping: Father I thank You that I am next in line for my blessings. I thank You for the outpouring of Your blessings on my neighbours. I celebrate their victories and breakthroughs and thank You that I am next in line for my blessings in Jesus' name I pray, amen.

Additional Food Sources: Luke 12:13 - 15, Romans 13:8-10, Ephesians 5:1-7

Have I been coveting or not celebrating my neighbors?

_____

_____

_____

_____

_____

_____

_____

_____

_____

_____

What steps can I take to show them more support and love?

_____

_____

_____

_____

_____

_____

_____

_____

_____

_____

_____

_____

Day 69

Food Source: John 5:5-6 NKJV

Food: *"Now a certain man was there who had an infirmity thirty-eight years. When Jesus saw him lying there, and knew that he already had been in that condition a long time, He said to him, "Do you want to be made well?""*

Nutrient: Be Patient

Digestion: There was a pool in Jerusalem called Bethseda. An angel usually went down into this pool a certain time to stir it so that whoever stepped into it first would be healed of whatever disease they had. This man was by the pool with his infirmity for 38 years because he had no one to put him in the pool. He told Jesus that every time he tried, someone stepped down before him. The text says a great multitude of sick people was there and no one was willing to put him in the pool because everyone wanted to be the one.

How many of us would throw in the towel after a year? How about 5 years? 10 years? This man was there before even Jesus was born but he had patience, he waited 38 years. He knew what he wanted and he was determined to get it! That place became his home because when Jesus showed up and asked him if he wanted to be made well and he said "yes", Jesus told him to take up his bed.

Many of us have been praying to God for some things and we don't see any results yet but today we need to become like this man by the pool and be patient. Some of us throw in the towel too easily and sometimes when we do, our breakthrough was right around the corner. James says that we should let patience have its perfect work because when it does we will become perfect and we won't lack anything. Love is also Patient.

Don't throw in that towel yet, God is still in control! Be Patient.

Grocery Shopping: Father I thank You for the reminder that we need to be patient. I don't know who this message is for today but I pray that they will allow patience to do its perfect work in them and that they will be rewarded with their breakthrough soon in Jesus' name I pray, amen.

Additional Food Sources: John 5:1-15, James 1:2-4, 1 Corinthians 13:4

What are the things that am I impatient about?

_____
_____
_____
_____
_____
_____
_____
_____
_____
_____
_____

How can I exercise more patience in these areas?

_____
_____
_____
_____
_____
_____
_____
_____
_____
_____
_____
_____

Day 70

Food Source: Matthew 25:41 NIV

Food: *"Then he will say to those on his left, 'Depart from me, you who are cursed, into the eternal fire prepared for the devil and his angels."*

Nutrient: Hell is Real, Repent

Digestion: Few days ago my devotion was **Seek and Find Him Today** and I told you that hell is real. I received a message being circulated sometime later, of an interview on YouTube which you can also find and watch. It is entitled: **Man was Taken by God to See Hell and Warn the World about sin!** I believe God wants me to remind you today that hell is real and that you should repent! Nobody knows when they will die. It could be the next second, minute, hour, day or year. Nobody knows!

There is no repentance in the grave. Once you die that is it, you have lost your opportunity and hell will be your reward. Our food is from the chapter where Jesus speaks of his return to separate the sheep (righteous) from the goat (unrighteous) and give them their reward. Whether you want to believe it or not that day will come. It is as real as gravity that you cannot see. If you jump it will pull you back to the ground, so is hell's eternal fire and heaven. Repent! Stop allowing the devil to deceive you!

Blessed are those who have not seen but yet believe. If you have not surrendered your life to Jesus, He is giving you another chance today to repent of your sins! Hell is real and it will be your reward if you don't repent! Seek the Lord while He can be found. If you die in your sin He cannot help you again. He already died for you. What more do you want Him to do, to prove that He loves you? If you are a backslider, He is giving you a second chance today! If you are a child of God and not living by God's Word you are in the same position and heading to hell! Hell is real my friend, repent now!

Grocery Shopping: Father You have been patient, You have warned us time and time again but some of us refuse to repent! So many have lost their lives by violence, disasters, accidents and sickness but You see it fit to give us another chance. Help us not to take Your mercy for granted any longer! Help us to recognize that hell is real and that if we do not repent while we are alive You can't help us. It is not Your desire for us to perish and as a result You are warning us again today. Help the person You are speaking to today to wake up, realize that they are heading for damnation and repent in Jesus' name I pray, amen.

Additional Food Sources: Matthew 25:31-46, John 20:29, Revelation 1:1-3, 20:7-10, Ecclesiastes 9:10

What are the things that I need to repent of today?

_____

_____

_____

_____

_____

_____

_____

_____

_____

_____

Begin to repent of them now and make a
commitment to serve Jesus.

_____

_____

_____

_____

_____

_____

_____

_____

_____

_____

_____

_____

Day 71

Food Source: I John 1:9 NKJV

Food: *"If we confess our sins, He is faithful and just to forgive us our sins and to cleanse us from all unrighteousness."*

Nutrient: Only Jesus Can Cleanse You

Digestion: Many unsaved struggle to surrender to Jesus because they think that they need to fix some things or cleanse themselves of all sins before they can come to Him. But this is not your job and the reality is you cannot cleanse yourself because you do not have the power to do so. This is Jesus' job. Our food says all we need to do is confess to Him. After we have done that He will forgive us because He is faithful and just. Then He will cleanse us from all unrighteousness. Man has a sinful nature and we will always be lured by our fleshly desires to sin. We therefore need the power of the Holy Spirit to help us to conquer our flesh and its desires. The Holy Spirit only dwells within you after you have been saved. You are saved when you confess with your mouth that Jesus is Lord and believe in your heart that God raised Him from the dead. When you get saved you will have a desire to be like Jesus which is a process that takes discipline.

By reading the Word of God you will know what He requires you to do and not to do. The Holy

211

Spirit teaches us, guides us and convicts us of our sins so that we can repent of them. All children of God sin after getting saved because cleansing is a process and it takes time to become like Jesus. If you have a bottle filled with dirt and water and you wish to get it clean you have to pour clean water in it for a while before all the dirt is displaced from it and it becomes clean. When we come to Jesus we are like that bottle of dirty water and only Jesus can cleanse us by pouring clean water into us through His Word. The beauty about being a Child of God however is the Grace that we have through Jesus. Once we sin, all we have to do is confess them and repent. He forgives us, cleanse us and He does not remember or haunt us with them, the devil does that. So don't be afraid! Come with all the dirt because only Jesus can cleanse you.

Grocery Shopping: Father, thank You for Your saving Grace. I recognize that only You can cleanse me, only You can fix the things that are not right in my life. I surrender to You today. Take me through Your cleansing process and help me to become like Christ in Jesus' name I pray, amen.

Additional Food Sources: Romans 10:9-13, 3:23, James 1:12-18, Galatians 5:16-25, Romans 8:1-2, 28-30, Hebrews 8:12.

If you are not saved, what are some of the things preventing you from accepting Jesus?

_____
_____
_____
_____
_____
_____
_____
_____
_____
_____

Do you believe that Jesus can cleanse you of these things? Write scriptures to support your belief and meditate on them.

_____
_____
_____
_____
_____
_____
_____
_____

Food Source: John 14:6 NKJV

Food: *"Jesus said to him, "I am the way, the truth, and the life. No one comes to the Father except through Me."*

Nutrient: Jesus is the Only Way

Digestion: Many people believe that they can live their lives the way they please and get to heaven but in our food Jesus was responding to Thomas, his disciple's question; how can we know the way? Jesus told him that "I am the way, the truth, and the life. No one comes to the Father except through Me." You cannot be saved any other way except through Jesus regardless of whatever justification you might want to come up with. It is just like the law of gravity, which I like to use as illustration because everyone has experienced it and should be able to relate to it. If you jump in the air there is no two ways about it, in a few seconds gravity will pull you to the ground. Try it now if you don't believe, jump and see what happens. Knowing this fact would you in your right mind go on top of a high rise building and jump? This fact, that Jesus exposed Thomas to in our food is a law just like gravity.

Mankind has discovered ways to defy gravity of course such as aerodynamics but it is a temporary solution and many planes have fallen from the sky. In the same way, mankind has found ways to convince themselves that there are other ways to be saved, other gods and other doctrines are okay. Jesus is the only way and the bible also tells us that *"every knee must bow and every tongue confess that Jesus Christ is Lord to the Glory of God the Father."* Are you going to jump off the building and see what happens even though you know the undisputed fact about gravity? Or are you going to accept the fact and save yourself the pain or sudden death? Jesus is the only way! Are you going to accept this fact and surrender to Him? Or are you going to try another way and perish?

Grocery Shopping: Father I acknowledge that Jesus is the only way to You. You said in Your Word that a fool despise wisdom. I don't wish to be a fool; I want to accept Your way. Help me to cast down every argument and high thing that exalts itself against the knowledge of God and bring every thought into captivity to the obedience of Christ in Jesus' name I pray, amen.

Additional Food Sources: Philippians 2:5-11, John 10:7-10, 1 Timothy 2:1-7, Proverbs 1:7, 2 Corinthians 10:4-6

What questions do I have about Jesus that causes me to doubt that He is the way?

_____
_____
_____
_____
_____
_____
_____
_____
_____
_____
_____
_____
_____

What steps can I take to get the answers to clarify these questions so that I can surrender to Jesus?

_____
_____
_____
_____
_____
_____
_____
_____
_____
_____

Day 73

Food Source: Jeremiah 29:11 NIV

Food: *"For I know the plans I have for you,"* *declares the Lord, "plans to prosper you and not to harm you, plans to give you hope and a future."*

Nutrient: God's Plan is to Prosper You

Digestion: Some time ago I struggled with the idea of selling my car because in my limited mental capacity I thought I needed to sell it to pay off some debts. I thought I needed to buy a cheaper car at one point but I rebuked the idea and the devil and told him that he will not rob me of anything God has blessed me with. I knew what our food is saying, that God's plan is always to prosper me and never to harm me. I knew His desire was for me to have a bright and fulfilled future.

When God told me to upgrade I began to move towards it but I was still limited by my mental capacity and thought I had to sell the car in order to upgrade but He approved the loan without me having to do that. I was told by the bank that I had to sell the car and pay off another loan before I was qualified for this loan. I worried for a second that I was not getting a buyer for the car but then God said to me don't sell it, rent it. So instead He gave me another source of income. I eventually sowed that car into God's kingdom which was one

217

of my best investments. His plan is to do what? Prosper you! Not to what? Harm you!

I don't know what the devil has been whispering in your ears but I am telling you today that the devil is a liar! You are royal priesthood and the apple of God's eyes! The devil is the one telling you that you are good for nothing! God wants you to be healthy, it is the devil telling you that you are going to be sick forever and die! You can achieve anything in life that you want through Christ; it is the devil telling you that you are a failure!

Every negative thought and fear is coming from the devil because God tells us to keep our mind positive and He has not given us a spirit of fear but of power, love and a sound mind! God wants to give you eternal life but the devil wants you to perish with him in hell. God's plan is for you to prosper my friend!

Grocery Shopping: Father I thank You for the plans that You have for my life, plans to prosper me and to give me hope and a future, not to harm me. Help me to acknowledge this fact and face life with boldness and confidence knowing that You are a God who is Faithful to Your Word and You will never leave me nor forsake me in Jesus' name I pray, amen.

Additional Food Sources: Philippians 4:8, John 10:10, 2 Timothy 1:7, Psalm 112, 118:17, 2 Peter 1:2-4, Luke 21:33

What lies has the devil whispered in your ears concerning your prosperity? Rebuke them.

_____
_____
_____
_____
_____
_____
_____
_____
_____
_____
_____
_____

Find promises that God has made in His Word concerning you and meditate on them.

_____
_____
_____
_____
_____
_____
_____
_____
_____

Day 74

Food Source: Luke 10:36-37 NKJV

Food: *"So which of these three do you think was neighbor to him who fell among the thieves?" And he said, "He who showed mercy on him." Then Jesus said to him, "Go and do likewise."*

Nutrient: Be a Good Samaritan

Digestion: A lawyer, an expert in the Mosaic Law was testing Jesus by asking Him what he shall do to inherit eternal life. Jesus asked him, what is written in the law? Part of his response was to love your neighbor as yourself. He further wanted to justify himself so he asked Jesus, who is my neighbor? Jesus responded by telling him the parable of the Good Samaritan with the aim of making him think and bring about a charge in his behavior.

In this story a man was robbed, beaten and left to die on his way from Jerusalem to Jericho. Two persons who were expected to assist, a priest and a Levite, servants of God, just passed by without helping. An enemy however, a Samaritan was the one who helped the man by nursing his wounds, taking him to the doctor and paid the expenses. Samaritans and Jews usually despise each other. After telling this story Jesus asked the lawyer the question in our food who was neighbor to this man? He responded, the one who showed him mercy. He was instructed by Jesus to go and do like the Samaritan.

Our neighbor is not just the person living beside us, but anyone in need of help or kindness and anyone who offers such help and kindness as demonstrated here. God wants us to love our neighbours as ourselves; it is a requirement to inherit eternal life. It is the solution to the crime and violence in our nations because love covers a multitude of sins. The bible says that we should not withhold good from those to whom it is due when it is in the power of our hands to do so. Do not pass that person in need today, be a Good Samaritan.

Grocery Shopping: Father I thank You for Your love. Cause it to stir up compassion within me today. Help me not to be like the priest who went on the other side and pass the man in need of help or like the Levite who went over and looked then pass by. Help me to be Good Samaritans today who will extend help to those in need, loving my neighbors as myself in Jesus' name I pray, amen.

Additional Food Sources: Luke 10:25-37, 1 Peter 4:8-10, Proverbs 3:27-30

Have I been a Good Samaritan? If not who can I help today?

_____

_____

_____

_____

_____

_____

_____

_____

_____

_____

_____

In what ways can I be helpful to these persons on a daily basis?

_____

_____

_____

_____

_____

_____

_____

_____

_____

_____

Day 75

Food Source: Psalms 14:1 NKJV

Food: *"The fool has said in his heart, "There is no God." They are corrupt, They have done abominable works, There is none who does good."*

Nutrient: **The Fool Says, "There is no God"**

Digestion: There are many people who do not believe that there is a God, they are called atheists. David says that they are fools because the fool has said in his heart, "There is no God." I believe in God not just because of what I have read or was taught but because I have experienced Him and have had several encounters with Him in my life and I have proven His Word to be true. Everyone has the right to believe what they wish and are given freedom of choice. But these beliefs and choices do not change the facts about God, who He is, what He has done and what He is going to do. An important fact is that everything in existence is capable of proof. The reality is, God is not afraid to show them that He is real. He has already revealed Himself to many because His Word says that every knee shall bow and every tongue shall confess to God.

The lack of belief in God has caused them to become evil in their thoughts. The enemy places his thoughts in their mind, making them to

223

believe that it's their thoughts. Isn't it interesting that the Word "evil" can be derived from his name, "devil" by just removing the "d"? Isn't it also interesting that you only need to add another "o" to God to get "good"? The reality is if you are not serving God you are serving the devil because they are the two forces acting in the world, good and evil.

What can we believers do? Pray for them; plant a seed of wisdom in their hearts when we can, water it and be patient for it to germinate because Jesus said if He be lifted up from this earth He will draw all people unto Him. Jesus was crucified, buried, resurrected from the dead on the third day and has ascended into heaven. He is now in the process of drawing them to Him. He also said, in the last days He will pour out his Spirit upon all flesh. There is still hope for the fools; God will reveal Himself to them when the time is right and grant them repentance so that they can be saved.

Grocery Shopping: Father, I am happy that You are the same yesterday, today and forevermore. Regardless of our beliefs and choices You are still God and evil only has a season to prevail in the earth. Speak to the hearts of Your people today. I pray that You will reveal yourself to those who are in doubt and need to see in order to believe. Bless those who have not seen but have believed in You.

Keep them rooted and grounded in Your Word in Jesus' name I pray, amen.

Additional Food Sources: Romans 14:11-13, John 12:32, Joel 2:28, Psalm 10, 53:1

Do you doubt that there is a God? List the reasons you have these doubt. If you have no doubts list the reasons why.

_____

_____

_____

_____

_____

_____

_____

_____

_____

_____

Ask God to reveal himself to you and prove that He is real. Write what He has revealed to you and share it with someone.

_____

_____

_____

_____

_____

_____

Day 76

Food Source: Psalms 100:4 NKJV

Food: *"Enter into His gates with thanksgiving, And into His courts with praise. Be thankful to Him, and bless His name."*

Nutrient: Glorify God with Thanksgiving & Testimony

Digestion: One of the things that I have learned about God is that He loves to be glorified. This is one of the reasons I believe He chose so many characters who thought they were inferior in the bible to do His work such as Moses, David, Gideon, Paul etc. He used these men because in their natural state they could not accomplish the task at hand and therefore needed to rely totally on Him. After the task was accomplished they had no choice but to glorify God.

One of the things that I did before I actually bought my new car was buy two license plate holders that would glorify God. One says: "Real Men Love Jesus" and the other: "Jesus, Don't leave Earth Without Him." The dealer would not put my plates on the car because their policy is to give me their plates to advertise their business. I was adamant that God will be glorified for His blessings on me so the first thing I did was to change the plates when I got home that day.

God demands His glory from us and He deserves it. Two of the ways that we can glorify God are: (1) Be thankful - we should be thankful in all things, not just in good times but also in bad times because even though you are going through a bad season you are still alive. Enter in His gates with thanksgiving, be thankful unto Him and bless His name. When you are thankful it moves God to do greater things for you. 10 Lepers were healed but one decided to return to Jesus to give thanks. The leper who returned to give thanks was not just healed but he was made whole.

(2) We must testify - The Words of our testimony help us to overcome. When we testify of God's goodness towards us, we glorify Him and cause others to increase their faith and also glorify Him. Regardless of your situation today, if you can read this then you need to glorify God with thanksgiving and testify about something He has done for you.

Grocery Shopping: Father You deserve the glory and the honor. If we should begin to testify of Your goodness towards us it would be a never ending story. I take the time just to say thank You today, for life. (Begin to list some things that you are thankful for today). I will testify of these things to others so that You will be glorified, in Jesus' name I pray, amen.

Additional Food Sources: Psalm 100:1-5, Psalm 116:17-19, 1 Thessalonians 5:18, Luke 17:11-19, Revelation 12:11

What are some of the things that I can be thankful for and testify about?

_____
_____
_____
_____
_____
_____
_____
_____
_____
_____
_____

What are the ways that I can glorify God?

_____
_____
_____
_____
_____
_____
_____
_____
_____
_____

Day 77

Food Source: I Kings 3:9 NKJV

Food: *"Therefore give to Your servant an understanding heart to judge Your people, that I may discern between good and evil. For who is able to judge this great people of Yours?"*

Nutrient: Seek Wisdom First Part 1:

Desire Wisdom

Digestion: Solomon inherited the throne of his father David and became King of Israel. God appeared to him at a place named Gibeon in a dream and asked him what he wanted from God. Solomon's request in our food was a heart of understanding, wisdom to Judge the people of Israel. His request pleased God because he did not ask for wealth or the life of his enemies. Therefore God also gave him a bonus of wealth and honor and his request, a unique wisdom.

Wisdom according to **Napoleon Hill in Outwitting the Devil** is the ability to relate yourself to nature's laws as to make them serve you and the ability to relate yourself to other people so as to gain their harmonious, willing cooperation in helping you to make life yield whatever you demand of it. Solomon knew that this was an important quality that he needed to be a great leader. He also discovered that if you have wisdom it will make life yield whatever you

229

demand of it and therefore he concluded that we should get wisdom first because it is the principal thing.

According to Napoleon Hill, wisdom however only comes to people who habitually think positive and have a desire to gain wisdom. People are not born with wisdom but the ability to think and they can think their way into wisdom as time lapses. When a baby for example is born he cannot talk but is born with the ability to talk. Exposure to persons talking to him on a daily basis causes him to develop the desire to talk. As time goes by he tries to talk and makes sounds until he gets the first Word out and eventually begins to talk. People can only give you knowledge but you must have a desire for wisdom to acquire it because wisdom comes from God. Do you want wisdom today? The first step is to develop a desire for wisdom.

Grocery Shopping: Father, I am thankful for the example of the wisest man, King Solomon. You gave him a request and he used it to ask for wisdom. Help us to follow this example. Wisdom will give us everything else that we demand of life so give us the desire to seek wisdom first so that we can make the knowledge that we have acquired, gain its power. Help us to apply the laws of nature and help us to develop influence so that we can gain and utilize the assistance of people to make life yield what we demand of it in Jesus' name I pray, amen.

Additional Food Sources: 1 Kings 3:5-15, Proverbs 4:7-9

Have you ever desired wisdom? Do you recognize the need for wisdom?

_____

_____

_____

_____

_____

_____

_____

_____

_____

_____

_____

How can I increase my desire for wisdom?

_____

_____

_____

_____

_____

_____

_____

_____

_____

_____

Day 78

Food Source: Proverbs 9:10 NKJV

Food: *"The fear of the LORD is the beginning of wisdom, And the knowledge of the Holy One is understanding."*

Nutrient: **Seek Wisdom First Part 2: Surrender to God, the Source of Wisdom**

Digestion: Before I became a Christian I had the wrong concept about so many things in life, marriage, love, sin etc. I was basically in darkness until I surrendered my life to Christ. When I did, my eyes began to open and I started seeing the light. Things I use to enjoy doing I started despising. As I got deeper in the Word of God, my understanding increased and my desire for wisdom increased.

Our food says, the fear of the Lord is the beginning of wisdom. Even though you desire wisdom, you will not begin to gain wisdom until you become a child of God. Knowledge of God opens your understanding and helps you to convert your knowledge to wisdom through its application. The bible was written by the Holy Spirit through men. Because He is the author, only He can teach us certain truths about the bible.

We therefore need the guidance of the Holy Spirit to fully understand the scriptures. The Holy Spirit only dwells within us when we surrender our lives to Jesus and repent of our sins. So after you have developed a desire for wisdom, the second step to getting wisdom is to surrender your life to the source of wisdom and repent of your sins. When you have done so, he will illuminate you with all truths and you will begin to gain wisdom. If you are a child of God and lack wisdom then you need to move to the third step, praying for wisdom. If you have not surrendered your life to Jesus Christ then you need to take this step today because it may be preventing you from gaining wisdom.

Grocery Shopping: Father I acknowledge that surrendering to You is the beginning of wisdom. I want to walk out of darkness and into light. Help me to make the decision today and begin the process of gaining wisdom. Open my eyes and my ears and help me to apply my heart unto wisdom in Jesus' name I pray, amen.

Additional Food Sources: Job 28:28, Psalm 111:10, Proverbs 1:7, Ecclesiastes 12:13, 2 Timothy 3:16-17, 2 Corinthians 4:6

What lessons did I learn from this message?

_____
_____
_____
_____
_____
_____
_____
_____
_____
_____
_____
_____
_____
_____

What are my action plans?

_____
_____
_____
_____
_____
_____
_____
_____
_____
_____
_____
_____

Day 79

Food Source: James 1:5 NIV

Food: *"If any of you lacks wisdom, you should ask God, who gives generously to all without finding fault, and it will be given to you."*

Nutrient: Seek Wisdom First Part 3:

Lack wisdom? Pray for it

Digestion: The final step to gaining wisdom that I want to look at is Praying for wisdom if you lack it.

I never knew that I lacked wisdom on financial matters until I read **'Rich Dad Poor Dad' by Robert Kiyosaki.** This book opened my eyes and placed me on the path of gaining wisdom by transforming my mind. I started to pray for wisdom and it did come, in proportions I didn't even expect. Indeed the fear of the Lord is the beginning of wisdom because that's when I started to gain wisdom, when I surrendered my life to Jesus Christ and began to pray for wisdom.

James says in our food that we should pray for wisdom if we lack it. He further stated in the verses that follow that we must have unwavering faith when we ask because if we don't we will not receive from God. So once more we see the importance of faith when praying to God, without faith it is impossible to please God. We should seek wisdom first instead of wealth because as Solomon demonstrated wisdom attracts wealth and honor. Wealth without wisdom in most if not all cases lead to misery and destruction. Lack wisdom? Pray for it with unwavering faith. Desire + Jesus + Prayer = Wisdom

Grocery Shopping: Father, I have realized that wisdom is the principal thing and that I need to seek it first. Give me the desire for wisdom and help me to surrender my life to You the source of wisdom. Lord I acknowledge that I lack wisdom and therefore I come to You in faith today, asking that You will grant me wisdom in Jesus' name I pray, amen.

Additional Food Sources: James 1:5-8, Proverbs 2:1-22, Hebrews 11:6

Have you ever prayed for wisdom? Make your request now.

_____
_____
_____
_____
_____
_____
_____
_____
_____
_____
_____

What steps do I to take to gain wisdom?

_____
_____
_____
_____
_____
_____
_____
_____
_____
_____
_____

Day 80

Food Source: Psalms 100:3 NKJV

Food: *"Know that the LORD, He is God; It is He who has made us, and not we ourselves; We are His people and the sheep of His pasture."*

Nutrient: **He Made Us, He Owns Us**

Digestion: Many of us live our lives without regard for God. We act as if God is obligated to us and we have all the time in the world to do what we want and then give God what is left of our lives when we are good and ready. But today God wants to remind us that He has loaned us His breath and He can take it back whenever He pleases because He is God. It is He who has made us, and not we ourselves; We are His people and the sheep of His pasture.

I bought a house so I own it. No one can tell me what to do with it because it is mine. Because He made us, He owns us. He is ever merciful and extends His Grace to us by giving us free will and freedom of choice. But as Solomon concluded after using his wisdom and great wealth to explore everything under the sun, the duty of man is to serve God. He says that we are His people and the sheep of His pasture. This means that He is our shepherd and the good shepherd takes care of His sheep. He also gave His life for His sheep.

The important character of the sheep is that the sheep follows its shepherd. Are you following your shepherd or are you being a goat instead of a sheep? A goat usually does its own thing unlike the sheep that follows the shepherd. A day is coming however when Jesus is going to return to separate the sheep from the goats. Which side will you be on when he returns? How long will you take your borrowed time and breath for granted? Do you know when God will want His breath back? Maybe if we did we would stop wasting time and do the right thing today. But shouldn't that uncertainty have the same effect?

Grocery Shopping: Father, You are God. We acknowledge that we didn't make ourselves but You did and You have a purpose for our lives. Help us to realize that tomorrow is not guaranteed because You can take back Your breath from us at any time, no one knows the hour. Help this uncertainty to help us to make the right decision today and begin to serve You as sheep in your pasture, in Jesus' name I pray, amen.

Additional Food Sources: John 10:11-18, Ecclesiastes 12:13, Matthew 25:31-33, John 3:16

What lessons did I learn from this message?

_____
_____
_____
_____
_____
_____
_____
_____
_____
_____
_____

What are my action plans?

_____
_____
_____
_____
_____
_____
_____
_____
_____
_____
_____

Day 81

Food Source: Nehemiah 8:10 NKJV

Food: *"Then he said to them, "Go your way, eat the fat, drink the sweet, and send portions to those for whom nothing is prepared; for this day is holy to our Lord. Do not sorrow, for the joy of the LORD is your strength."*

Nutrient: **The Joy of the Lord Is Your Strength**

Digestion: Many of us live our lives in despair. We worry, get depressed, procrastinate and get stuck in the land of hopelessness because we keep our minds dwelling on negative thoughts. The things that we did not achieve, the mistakes we made, the opportunities that passed us by, the people who hurt us, the things we want and can't afford and the pain we are feeling. We stay in this state so long that we forget the positive things in our lives and feel like giving up. Today, like Nehemiah was saying in our food to the Israelites after they had read them the Laws of God and they were mourning, this day is holy to our Lord. It is time to stop mourning, time to eat and be merry and share with those who don't have because the joy of the Lord is your strength. It is time to get out of the land of despair. Your situation will not change until you start doing what is necessary to change it.

Renew your mind; substitute all those negative thoughts with positive ones. I am blessed and highly favored, I am an overcomer, I will not die but live and declare the works of the Lord, I will not suffer or beg bread because God will supply all my needs according to His riches in glory. There is hope because God's plan is to give me a future and a hope that eyes have not seen, ears have not heard nor has it entered into the heart of man the things that God has prepared for me because I love Him. Exalt God above every negative situation because everything in life has a season and time and chance happens to every man. Though you may be weeping now, your joy will come soon because your season is changing. You have the power to change it. Be grateful for what God has already done for you, worship Him in spite of the despair and you will please Him and give Him joy and this joy will become your strength.

Grocery Shopping: Father, I thank You for Your strength today. I am going through the land of despair because of life's struggles and challenges but help me to cross that border and step into the land of hope and prosperity because You are God and nothing is impossible for You. You are Faithful to Your Word and You deserve my praise regardless of my situation. I exalt You above every situation today and give You all the glory because my season is changing in Jesus' name I pray, amen.

Additional Food Sources: Philippians 4:8,19, Psalm 118:17, 37:25, 30:5, Jeremiah 29:11, 1 Corinthians 2:9, Ecclesiastes 3:1-8, 9:11

What situations do I have that causes me to be in despair?

_____
_____
_____
_____
_____
_____
_____
_____
_____
_____

What can I do to get out of this state?

_____
_____
_____
_____
_____
_____
_____
_____
_____
_____

Day 82

Food Source: James 1:22-24 NLT

Food: *"But don't just listen to God's Word. You must do what it says. Otherwise, you are only fooling yourselves. For if you listen to the Word and don't obey, it is like glancing at your face in a mirror. You see yourself, walk away, and forget what you look like."*

Nutrient: Don't Just Hear the Word, Do it!

Digestion: Many of people, like me at one point before I actually got saved, grew up in church, go to church on a regular basis, hear the Word regularly and know the Word of God or all of the above. But what impact has it had on your life? Before I became a Christian there were many things I never did or would never do like stealing because the Word of God says Thou shalt not steal.

When we hear the Word of God it should bring some sort of transformation in our lives. It actually has the power to do that. Paul says in his letter to Timothy that all scriptures are given by inspiration of God and is profitable for doctrine, for reproof, for correction in righteousness. So you see if we allow it, the Word of God will teach us how to live and correct us when we falter.

Our food says that we should not only listen to the Word of God but we should also do what it says because if we don't then we are fooling ourselves and we are like the man who looks in the mirror at his face and the moment he walks away, forgets what he looks like. We should hide the Word of God in our hearts when we hear them and let them become our guideline for living. When we do this we will please God and He will bless us. Don't just hear the Word but do what it says.

Grocery Shopping: Father I thank You for giving me the Grace to share Your Word with Your people on a daily basis. Help us not to just hear the Word but do what it says. Help us to hide Your Word in our hearts that we will be directed and corrected by it and as a result, not sin against You in Jesus' name I pray, amen.

Additional Food Sources: 2 Timothy 3:16-17, Matthew 7:21-27, Romans 2:12-16, Psalm 119:11

What Word have I been hearing?

_____

_____

_____

_____

_____

_____

_____

_____

_____

_____

_____

How can I apply this Word in my life?

_____

_____

_____

_____

_____

_____

_____

_____

_____

_____

_____

Day 83

Food Source: Genesis 2:2-3 KJV

Food: *"And on the seventh day God ended his work which he had made; and he rested on the seventh day from all his work which he had made. And God blessed the seventh day, and sanctified it: because that in it he had rested from all his work which God created and made."*

Nutrient: **Rest is Necessary**

Digestion: One day I came home feeling like an energizer bunny and decided I was going to cook some carrots to make some carrot punch. I sat down in my chair and I don't even know when that energizer bunny became a sleeping bunny. I was deceiving myself because my body was tired and had other plans. Luckily the Lord woke me up, when I rushed to the kitchen my pot of carrots looked like a pot of charcoal and the house was saturated with its burning aroma.

Rest is necessary my friends! The all-powerful God as seen in our food created the earth in 6 days and rested on the 7th day from all His work. This was His demonstration and example to us that we need to rest our body. I felt energized that night but my body was tired and responded in that way by taking its rest. If we do not rest our body it can be catastrophic. Many of us try to kill work by working 7 days per week but we can't kill

247

work, work is rather the killer and we are actually killing ourselves instead.

Our body was designed to rest and that is why we sleep. If we don't rest, then our body will shut down and/or it will give us other countless signs in the form of illness. The manifestations of not having enough rest are too much to be outlined in this devotional, therefore I encourage you to research why we need to rest. Slow down my friend, take some time and rest. God is an immortal Spirit and He rested; we are mortals, our body will give up. Rest is necessary.

Grocery Shopping: Father we thank You for Your example and reminder today that we need to rest. Cause us to have sweet, peaceful sleep that rejuvenates us. Help us not only to sleep but to rest our minds from the stress and the cares of this life and find peace of mind in Jesus' name I pray, amen.

Additional Food Sources: Exodus 20:9-11, 31:17, Psalm 4:8

How much rest do I get each day?

_____
_____
_____
_____
_____
_____
_____
_____
_____
_____

Is this enough rest for my body? If not, what steps can I take to get more rest?

_____
_____
_____
_____
_____
_____
_____
_____
_____
_____
_____
_____
_____

Food Source: Galatians 6:7 NKJV

Food: *"Do not be deceived, God is not mocked: for whatever a man sows, that he will also reap."*

Nutrient: You Will Reap What You Sow

Digestion: We all have high expectations for life. Some of us have long term and short term goals and visions for our lives. The key principle to achieving these however is highlighted in our food today. Whatever a man sows, that he will also reap. Those of you who are familiar with farming know that this is a fact for the farmer. If he plants corn it is just not possible for him to reap peas. Corn sown, produces a harvest of corn. The principle remains true for every other aspect of life. A man who lives a life of crime without repentance will no doubt end up dead or in prison.

We are who we are because of what we think and what we do. There is no action without us first having a thought. That is why it is said, whatever your mind conceives you can achieve. If your thoughts are negative then it will always produce negative results. If your thoughts are positive then you will always produce positive results.

This means that we need to be careful of the thoughts that we dwell on. You should always keep your thoughts positive. Because you will reap what you sow. A good principle outlined by *Napoleon Hill* to adopt is, offering service equivalent to the value of that which you demand of life, and plant that seed first. Happiness comes only from giving useful service to others and adding value to the lives of others. You must sow before you can reap and you will reap what you sow.

Grocery Shopping: Father I acknowledge that whatever I sow is what I will reap in this life. Help me to sow good and not evil, positive and not negative seeds. Help me to have a heart like Yours and do all the good I can to add value to the lives of my neighbours because this will bring true happiness in Jesus' name I pray, amen.

Additional Food Sources: Galatians 6:6-10, Philippians 4:8, Proverbs 3:27

What would I like to achieve in life?

_____
_____
_____
_____
_____
_____
_____
_____
_____
_____
_____
_____

What seeds have I been sowing? Will these seeds help me to achieve my goals?

_____
_____
_____
_____
_____
_____
_____
_____
_____
_____
_____
_____

Day 85

Food Source: Psalms 1:2-3 NKJV

Food: *"But his delight is in the law of the LORD, And in His law he meditates day and night. He shall be like a tree Planted by the rivers of water, That brings forth its fruit in its season, Whose leaf also shall not wither; And whatever he does shall prosper."*

Nutrient: **Delight, Meditate, Connect and Prosper (DMCaP)**

Digestion: One of the first chapters I learnt as a child growing up was Psalm 1. I began to see the true meaning of it only a few months after studying Hermeneutics and learnt how to interpret the scriptures. Indeed, it is good for us to study to show ourselves approved and rightly divide the Word of truth. It is never too late to learn. In order to grow we must continue to study so we must decide to do so until we die.

These two verses in our food stood out to me and three things came alive:

1. A smart person spends his/her time reading the Word of God and thinks deeply on it day and night.
2. Because he/she does this, he/she becomes like a tree planted by the rivers of water. A tree needs water to bear fruit. The fact that it is planted by the river means that it gets

253

water all the time and as a result its leaf cannot wither. This person is compared to this tree. This meditation on the Word will connect him/ her to God, the source who will always supply all that he/she needs to bear fruit and he/she will not die spiritually.

3. Because he/she has this connection with God and is being watered, he/she must bear fruit (be successful), cannot wither or become stagnant in life and whatever he/she does will prosper. This tells me that prosperity is linked to delighting in God and meditating on his Word.

Delight causes **m**editation, meditation cause **c**onnection **a**nd connection cause **p**rosperity (**DMCaP**). Start to DMCaP today my friend.

Grocery Shopping: Father I thank You for the illumination of the Holy Spirit which brings clarity to Your Word. I pray that Your wisdom will begin to illuminate the person reading this devotion today and cause them to **DMCaP** in Jesus' name I pray, amen.

Additional Food Sources: Psalm 1, Psalm 37:4, 2 Timothy 2:15

How much time do I spend in the Word of God?

_____
_____
_____
_____
_____
_____
_____
_____
_____
_____
_____
_____

What verses have I been meditating on?

_____
_____
_____
_____
_____
_____
_____
_____
_____
_____
_____
_____
_____

Day 86

Food Source: Ecclesiastes 3:1 NKJV

Food: *"To everything there is a season, A time for every purpose under heaven:"*

Nutrient: Your Season Will Change

Digestion: Many of us are going through some bad seasons in our lives, financially, emotionally, mentally, spiritually or even physically but according to our food today that season cannot remain forever because everything has a season and therefore your season must change. Though it would be ideal to always be happy, we will not always be happy because there is a time for every purpose.

You can rest assured that though you may be struggling financially now a season of abundance is promised, though you may be sad now, a season of joy is coming, though you may be depressed now a season of peace and contentment is coming, though you may be weak in spirit, God has a fresh anointing that is waiting for you and though you may be sick, a season of good health is coming.

There are some seasons in our lives that change automatically like autumn, summer, spring and winter. Some seasons however change manually, if you don't do what is necessary to change them, they won't change. The good news is, you have the power to change them. A financial season is one such season. Many of us are waiting on God to give us heavenly money but God has already given us the ability before we were born to create our wealth, all we need sometimes is a little determination, commitment, perseverance and faith.

God is waiting on you my friend. Quit worrying about the automatic seasons today, change the manual seasons that you have the power to change.

Grocery Shopping: Father I thank you that my season will change because You created a season for everything. Help me to be patient on You to change the seasons that are automatic. Give me the courage to change the manual seasons and the wisdom to know the difference between the two seasons in Jesus' name I pray, amen.

Additional Food Sources: Ecclesiastes 3:1-8, 17, 8:6, Deuteronomy 8:18

What season have I been experiencing?

_____
_____
_____
_____
_____
_____
_____
_____
_____
_____
_____

Is there something that I need to do to change it?

_____
_____
_____
_____
_____
_____
_____
_____
_____
_____
_____

Day 87

Food Source: Matthew 6:10 NKJV

Food: *"Your kingdom come. Your will be done On earth as it is in heaven."*

Nutrient: Let God's Will Be Done

Digestion: One of the worse things to do is to fight God's Will for your life. This conclusion can be drawn by examining the lives of many characters in the bible that disobeyed God and the result: Adam and Eve, the Israelites, Moses and Jonah to name a few. Adam and Eve, they ate the forbidden fruit and brought sin into the world and the effect of that is just catastrophic. Men have to work hard until they die to eat bread and women bear great pain during pregnancy and delivery. Yes, that's the result of their disobedience.

You are fighting a hopeless battle because as our food says, His will must be done on earth as it is in heaven. Jesus understood and demonstrated this. I believe that Jesus did not want to go through the agony of dying on a cross. He went to the Mount of Olives and prayed 3 times, the same prayer asking God if it is possible to take the cup away from Him. He was in agony and prayed until his sweat became like drops of blood. But He submitted and said, "Nevertheless not my will, but Yours be done."

This is the place that we have to get to in order to experience His joy. We have to reach the place where His will and our will are one and there is no wrestling. When we get to this place, prayer becomes more effective because God will grant us our desires as they are also His desires. Jesus knew He had to die, He could have saved Himself all that trouble but prayer was necessary for His strength to complete His mission. It is human nature to always seek a way out of God's Will. But let us become submissive to God and Let His will be done in our lives today.

Grocery Shopping: Father I acknowledge that Your will must be done on this earth as it is in heaven. Help me to be submissive to Your will today because I realize also that when my will is in sync with your will prayer will be easy and more effective. Direct my path, show me Your will and let it be done in my life today in Jesus' name I pray, amen.

Additional Food Sources: Genesis 3:9-19, Luke 22:39-44

Which of God's Will for my life have I been
wrestling with?

_____
_____
_____
_____
_____
_____
_____
_____
_____
_____
_____

What can I do to let His will be done?

_____
_____
_____
_____
_____
_____
_____
_____
_____
_____
_____
_____

Day 88

Food Source: I Timothy 5:23 NKJV

Food: *"No longer drink only water, but use a little wine for your stomach's sake and your frequent infirmities."*

Nutrient: Drink a Little Wine with Caution

Digestion: Many people are of the opinion that believers should not drink wine but on the contrary Paul was encouraging Timothy in our food to not only drink water but a little wine for the stomach's sake and the frequent infirmities (illnesses) which suggest that wine has some virtue of healing for the body. The first miracle that Jesus did was to turn water into wine at the wedding which means that He also does not discourage its drinking.

Self-control is very important in all that we do however and therefore we should not overly indulge to become drunk. In fact Paul also cautioned us in his letter to the Ephesians not to be drunk with excess wine but we should be filled with the Spirit. Solomon also cautioned us against this and said that if we are lead astray by wine then we are not wise.

Solomon later highlights some of the effects of overindulgence in wine. These are: distress, sorrow, contention, babbling, wound without cause and redness of eyes.

262

Interestingly he also forbids red wine, wine that gives its color in the cup or goes down smoothly because after you have had it, it will bite like a serpent and sting like a snake. It will cause your eyes to see strange things and you will say perverse things. Enjoy life with a little wine but exercise caution!

Grocery Shopping: Father we thank You for Your Word today which encourages us to drink a little wine to help heal our body. Help us to exercise caution in the type of wine that we drink and how much we intake so that we do not become drunk by it but help us to be filled with your spirit in Jesus' name I pray, amen.

Additional Food Sources: Ephesians 5:15-21, Proverbs 20:1, 23:29-35

When was the last time I had some wine?

_____
_____
_____
_____
_____
_____
_____
_____
_____
_____
_____

Am I exercising caution with my intake?

_____
_____
_____
_____
_____
_____
_____
_____
_____
_____
_____

Day 89

Food Source: Psalm 23:4 NKJV

Food: *"Yea, though I walk through the valley of the shadow of death, I will fear no evil; For You are with me; Your rod and Your staff, they comfort me."*

Nutrient: **Go Through the Valley, Don't Die There**

Digestion: Many of us are going through what the psalmist refer to in our food as the valley of the shadow of death in our lives. Your valley may be financial struggles, relationship with spouse, friends and family, mental struggle with self-worth, health issues, enemies who have risen against you without cause or any other negative situation in your life. You may feel like these situations are sucking the life out of you and you want to give up but God wants to let you know today that you are supposed to go through this valley and you will not die in it!

Even though you are going through this valley you need not to be afraid because God is with you and if God be with you then you must have victory, you must overcome. What you need to do is learn while you are in the valley, pray while you are in the valley, get closer to God in the valley, praise God in the valley and let His joy renew your strength in the valley. He is with you! Talk to Him

265

in the valley, cry out to Him in the valley, express your true feelings to Him in the valley, lift your faith and love Him even in the valley.

He will comfort you in your valley after you have done all these things because you trusted Him in your valley. Your valley is your test! Your valley is to make you stronger, increase your faith, change your path, get you closer to God and where He wants you to be. Your breakthrough is in your valley, your healing is in your valley, your deliverance is in your valley and the answer to your problems is also in your valley. Discover it! Don't die in your valley, you are meant to go through it.

Grocery Shopping: Father I thank You that even though I am going through my valley of the shadow of death You are with me. Because You are with me, I will have no fear but I will pass this test and go through this valley. I will not die in this valley! I command my breakthrough, my deliverance, my healing and the solutions to my problems to come forth in Jesus' name I pray, amen.

Additional Food Sources: Psalm 23

What valley am I going through?

_____
_____
_____
_____
_____
_____
_____
_____
_____
_____
_____

How am I learning from this valley experience?

_____
_____
_____
_____
_____
_____
_____
_____
_____
_____
_____
_____
_____
_____

Day 90

Food Source: I Samuel 15:22 NKJV

Food: *"So Samuel said: "Has the LORD as great delight in burnt offerings and sacrifices, As in obeying the voice of the LORD? Behold, to obey is better than sacrifice, And to heed than the fat of rams."*

Nutrient: **Obedience is God's Desire**

Digestion: The evil of the Amalekites towards Israel had gotten to God's attention and as a result He instructed King Saul to destroy all that they had and not to spare them. Saul however disobeyed God's command because he feared the people. He therefore allowed them to take the best of all their cattle and goods and he also spared their King Agag. When the prophet Samuel came to him and asked him why he had disobeyed and taken the plunder, his explanation was that the people took them to sacrifice to the Lord.

But in our food Samuel explained to Saul that it is better to obey God than make sacrifices to Him and to take heed to His Word than offer the fat of rams. Obedience is God's desire. As a result of his disobedience God rejected him as king and selected a man of his own heart, David. His throne was torn from him and he stopped hearing from God because Samuel never came back to him from that day.

God sought a man after His own heart because such a man will obey Him and take heed to His Word. All God wants is for us to obey Him and take heed to His Word, just like parents desire for their children to obey them because they know what is right and what is best for them. God knows everything about us, He has planned our whole lives with only prosperity in mind, He knows the future and He is Faithful to His Word.

For these reasons and my bad experiences when I disobey, I have learned to obey Him and take heed to His Word. Will you give God His desire today? Will you obey Him and take heed to His Word?

Grocery Shopping: Father, I know that Your desire is for me to obey and take heed to Your Word. Make it my desire to do so and help me to be committed to doing so in Jesus' name I pray, amen.

Additional Food Sources: 1 Samuel 13:14, 1 Samuel 15, Jeremiah 29:11

How have I been disobeying God?

_____
_____
_____
_____
_____
_____
_____
_____
_____
_____
_____
_____

What steps do I need to take to start obeying Him?

_____
_____
_____
_____
_____
_____
_____
_____
_____
_____

ABOUT THE AUTHOR

Clatin Williams was born in the Parish of Clarendon on May 5, 1985. He has a Bachelor of Science Degree in Construction Management from the University of Technology, Jamaica and is a Construction Manager by profession.

Clatin surrendered his life to the Lord and was baptized on April 28, 2013 at the Sandy Bay New Testament Church of God in Clarendon.

He was led by the Lord to Worship and Faith International Fellowship in July 2015 and has been a member since August 28, 2016. He serves faithfully as the Men's Ministry Secretary, teacher of membership 1 class, a cell group leader, a member of the evangelism team and a member of the WAFIF Academy of Excellence's school board.

Clatin is a graduate of the Courtney McLean School of Ministry, valedictorian for the graduating class Preaching 101, 2016.

He is a certified mentor with World Needs a Father and National Integrity Action/ MENFA International.

Clatin is passionate about the Word of God, His kingdom and transforming the lives of His people by sharing the knowledge and wisdom he gains as he goes along his journey.

Contact Clatin Williams at:
Telephone: 379-6962
Email: spiritualfoodclatin@gmail.com

Facebook:
https://www.facebook.com/spiritualfoodcw/

Instagram: spiritualfoodbyclatinwilliams

TOPIC INDEX

273

TOPIC	DAY	TOPIC	DAY
Endurance	58	Hard Work	24
Enemy	20	Healing	30
Escape	58	Heart	45, 56
Faith	9, 11, 30, 46, 48, 50, 60, 62, 79	Hell	67, 69
Fatherhood	51	Helping	7, 41, 74
Favor	13	Heritage	51
Fear	22	Hierarchy	55
Fighting	62	History	27
First Fruit	52	Holy Spirit	19
Fool	75	Homosexuals	31
Forget	59	Honesty	26
Forgiveness	3, 25, 29, 59	Honor	5, 38, 52
Friend	11	Husband	55
Fruit of the Spirit	19	Impossible Situations	9
Fulfillment	60	Jonathan	32
Fun	14	Joy	3, 7, 81
Giving	5, 52	Judgement	66
Goals	24	Judging	31
Goat	41, 80	Knock	63
God's Plan	73	Knowledge	20
God's Will	2, 87	Leadership	55
Good	7	Lies	26
Gravity	72	Light	42

TOPIC	DAY	TOPIC	DAY
Listen	82	Passion	42
Love	4, 16, 27, 32, 35, 51, 56, 57, 64, 68, 74	Patience	69
Marriage	15, 16, 17	Perseverance	46
Meditation	85	Planning	24
Mercy	3, 49	Positive Thoughts	21, 81, 8
Mind	21, 56	Possible	9
Motive	53	Potential	65
Multiply	6	Power	20
Needs	6, 41	Power of Agreement	15, 16
Negative Thoughts	21, 81, 84	Power of the Tongue	11, 14
Neighbor	27, 57, 68, 74	Praise	4
New	54	Prayer	29, 44, 7
Obedience	40, 82, 87, 90	Product	65
Obstacles	18	Proof	75
Offering	52	Prophecy	61, 62
Outwitting the Devil	20, 21, 22	Prosperity	24, 73, 8
Overcoming	11, 89	Provision	1
Parenting	10	Purpose	13, 15, 1
Partner	15, 16, 17	Reaping	84

TOPIC	DAY	TOPIC	DAY
Rejoice	46	Strong Tower	37
Relationship	12	Struggles	89
Remarriage	17	Supply	6
Repentance	3, 29, 37, 59, 66, 70, 71, 72, 78, 80	Surprise	64
Rest	83	Temptation	58
Righteous	33	Testament	57
Sacrifice	5,90	Testimony	76
Safe	37	Thankful	6
Salvation	31, 67, 70, 71, 72, 78	Thanksgiving	76
Season	81, 86	Time Management	39
Seed	6	Transformation	54
Seek	63, 67	Trials	46
Self-Worth	4	Troubles	33
Sheep	41, 80	Trust	1, 23, 26, 34, 47, 48
Shepherd	80	Truth	26
Sin	29, 59, 71	Unequally Yoked	15
Smile	3	Unity	43
Soul	56	Valley	89
Soulmate	16, 17	Verdict	44
Sowing	84	Vindication	18
Special	4	Vision	42
Storm	2	Way	72
Strength	23, 50, 81	Weakness	23

TOPIC	DAY	TOPIC	DAY
Wife	55	Word of God	36, 42, 82, 85, 90
Wine	88	Work	38
Wisdom	77, 78, 79	Worrying	8